**Making
soil and water
conservation work:
Scientific
and policy
perspectives**

Making soil and water conservation work: Scientific and policy perspectives

Edited by Daniel W. Halbach, C. Ford Runge, and William E. Larson

SOIL
CONSERVATION
SOCIETY
OF AMERICA

Soil Conservation Society of America
7515 Northeast Ankeny Road
Ankeny, Iowa 50021

Library of Congress Catalog Card Number 87-16412

ISBN 0-935734-16-3

$10.00

Library of Congress Cataloging-in-Publication Data

Main entry under title:

Making Soil and Water Conservation Work

  Based on papers from a conference held October 14-15,
1986, in St. Paul, Minnesota, and sponsored by the University
of Minnesota, Department of Agricultural and Applied
Economics, Department of Soil Science, and the Hubert H.
Humphrey Institute of Public Affairs.
  Includes bibliographies and index.
  1. Soil conservation—Government policy—United States—
Congresses. 2. Water conservation—Government policy—
United States—Congresses. 3. Soil conservation—United
States—Congresses. 4. Water conservation—United States—
Congresses. I. Halbach, Daniel W. II. Runge, C. Ford (Carlisle
Ford). III. Larson, William E., 1921-   . IV. University of Min-
nesota. Department of Agricultural and Applied Economics. V.
University of Minnesota. Department of Soil Science. VI.
Hubert H. Humphrey Institute of Public Affairs.
S624.A1M34 1987   333.73'16   87-16412
ISBN 0-935734-16-3

Contributors

James L. Arts
Land Resources Specialist, Wisconsin Department of Agriculture, Trade and Consumer Protection, Madison

Sandra S. Batie
Professor, Department of Agricultural Economics, Virginia Polytechnic Institute and State University, Blacksburg

Charles M. Benbrook
Executive Director, Board on Agriculture, National Research Council, Washington, D.C.

Norman A. Berg
Senior Advisor, American Farmland Trust, Washington, D.C.

John B. Braden
Associate Professor, Department of Agricultural Economics, University of Illinois, Champaign-Urbana

Michael R. Dicks
Agricultural Economist, National Resource Economics Division, Economic Research Service, U.S. Department of Agriculture, Washington, D.C.

Chris J. Johannsen
Director, Agricultural Data Network, Purdue University, West Lafayette, Indiana

Greg Larson
Program Specialist, Soil and Water Conservation Board, Minnesota Department of Agriculture, St. Paul

Peter J. Nowak
Soil and Water Conservation Specialist, Department of Rural Sociology, University of Wisconsin, Madison

Francis J. Pierce
Assistant Professor, Crop and Soil Sciences Department, Michigan State University, East Lansing

C. Ford Runge
Associate Professor, Department of Agricultural and Applied Economics, University of Minnesota, St. Paul

Steven J. Taff
Assistant Professor, Department of Agricultural and Applied Economics, University of Minnesota, St. Paul

Jim Vertrees
Agricultural Economist, Economic Analysis Staff, Office of the Assistant Secretary for Economics, U.S. Department of Agriculture, Washington, D.C.

Contents

Preface

Throughout the 1970s, world demand for U.S. grain caused major pressures on the natural resource endowment of our nation. Years of soil and water conservation efforts were lost to fencerow-to-fencerow production. With the decline of export markets beginning in 1980-1981, oversupply has become the norm. Yet strong interest in maintaining agricultural productivity and improved environmental quality continues.

A resurgence in soil conservation interest is exemplified by the Conservation Reserve Program of the 1985 farm bill and a variety of state-level programs. However, these and other efforts have been hampered by uncertainties over how best to target land for conversion from crop production to more conserving land uses. Recent modeling efforts have provided means for estimating changes in soil productivity due to erosion. These advances, along with modern soil surveys, provide the basis for greatly improved targeting procedures. Scientific advances must also be accompanied by local and national policy reforms for improved conservation programs to become a reality.

This book resulted from a two-day gathering of leading scientists, economists, and public policy experts, held October 14-15, 1986, in St. Paul, Minnesota. The formal papers and discussions provide excellent background information for improved conservation programs. We are most grateful to the authors and participants. Sponsored by the University of Minnesota Department of Agricultural and Applied Economics, Department of Soil Science, and the Hubert H. Humphrey Institute of Public Affairs, the conference involved the mutual efforts of many talented individuals. Conference staff support was provided by Betty Radcliffe and Yvonne Cheek of the Humphrey Institute and Judy Hughes and Janet Cardelli of the Department of Agricultural and Applied Economics. Financial support came from the Northwest Area Foundation of St. Paul, Minnesota. Special appreciation is expressed to Karl Stauber for the interest he has shown in this project.

Daniel Halbach
General Editor

Introduction

One question regularly confronts the soil and water conservation community: How do we apply scientific knowledge to improve conservation policy while recognizing political reality? This problem is captured by three interlinked adages: all politics is local; all conservation is local; all conservation is political. The difficult task of balancing the local and political interests of scientists, conservationists, and government servants led to the papers in this volume. Each paper reflects on this problem while charting a course for new and innovative approaches. Charting this course requires attention to the scientific, state, and federal issues confronting current soil and water conservation policy.

The changing scientific basis of conservation policy is most clearly reflected in the research success achieved by soil scientists in quantifying productivity losses due to soil erosion and the vulnerability of soils to these losses. While much remains to be done, the recent development of a "productivity index" as well as measures of soil resistance to erosion is an important step beyond older, more subjective measures. Their most important, current use is in targeting policy. They have already proven successful as the basis for the RIM (Reinvest in Minnesota) program, which targets soil and water conservation efforts according to the productivity of various lands and their capacity to resist erosion. The scientific papers in this volume document these efforts and indicate where further research and testing is needed.

The second main task of the volume is to assess current federal conservation efforts using the insights gained from this scientific information.

In spite of enthusiasm for the Conservation Reserve Program, improved targeting criteria could have resulted in lower costs and higher conservation benefits. Recent attempts to sweeten these benefits by paying farmers to take corn land out of production indicate the severe competition that exists between the CRP and federal commodity programs. Not only the CRP but a variety of other federal agricultural programs, including crop set-asides, would benefit from improved targeting so that lands deserving long-term retirement are not used instead to satisfy largely futile, year-to-year attempts to control supply. The result would be both better supply control and better conservation.

These issues are in the realm of politics, however, and are best addressed from a perspective that acknowledges the political difficulties of applying science to policy. The authors of the several papers addressing these issues acknowledge these difficulties, but share a conviction that they can now be overcome with the insights resulting from scientific research. Especially as federal budget constraints bind agricultural and conservation program spending, improved conservation targeting becomes not only a scientific virtue but an economic necessity.

The final perspective brought to bear by this volume is the role of the states. Federalism—the shared authority of state and federal governments—is nowhere more important than in environmental policy, where local information and initiative is crucial. As the aforementioned budget constraints bind federal initiatives ever more tightly, imaginative state programs will become increasingly important. The experience of Minnesota's RIM program, together with examples from Wisconsin and Illinois, provide ample evidence that states can not only complement but also improve on federal policies, perhaps showing the federal programs aspects of their future.

Together, scientific, federal, and state policy perspectives will all be necessary to translate new research into new policy. While this process is already underway, the papers in this volume can help push it along. We believe that innovative policies in soil and water conservation will benefit both the conservation community and the general public, for whom environmental quality may be the most important issue of the next century.

C. Ford Runge
and William E. Larson
Editors

Soil and water quality: A scientific perspective

1

Supply control, conservation, and budget restraint: Conflicting instruments in the 1985 farm bill

Steven J. Taff and C. Ford Runge

> Social policy has entered the stage in which the ambitiousness of government must be matched by analytic competence if the nation is to avoid a condition—more common elsewhere in the world than perhaps realized—in which the grandiosity of official pronouncement is equalled only by the absence of result.
>
> *Daniel Patrick Moynihan*

In the heat of legislative action, compromises are often made, the net effect of which is clear only as programs are implemented. The Food Security Act of 1985, the farm bill, is a good example of such unintended side effects. The cost of the bill was intentionally underestimated to ensure passage. Low market prices and high deficiency payments encouraged high levels of participation, making greater budget exposure an inevitable outcome. Recently reported cost overruns should come as no surprise, although their size has surprised even the most pessimistic analysts.

Few realized, however, that mandated acreage reductions for program crops, designed in large part to reduce budget exposure, might have other undesired consequences. One of the most important has been to undermine the cost-effectiveness of the Conservation Reserve Progam (CRP), mandated under a separate title of the bill.

Targets and instruments in agricultural policy

Although a wide variety of objectives are advanced for agricultural policy (the 1985 farm bill notes as least seven; the conservation title itself lists another seven), we are concerned with three of principal importance to Congress and the U.S. Department of Agriculture: (1) supply control, (2) conservation of marginal agricultural lands, and (3) budget discipline. The first two are explicit farm bill goals; the third was implicit throughout the debate. These program goals were intended to be met by two principal policy instruments (programs): acreage reductions and a conservation reserve. But the links between instruments and objectives were muddled at best.

Supply control was to be achieved in large part by the acreage reduction program (ARP), whereby eligibility for loan and deficiency payments is made conditional on reductions in acreage planted to program crops.[1] Although the intent is supply control, the main effect of ARPs is to reduce budget exposure by lowering the acreage on which program benefits are to be paid. The reason that ARPs generally fail to control supply—well-known to farmers but apparently not to policymakers—will be explored in greater detail below. Budget savings, however, are more assured. With July 1986 prices, loan rates, and deficiency payments, 1986 costs for the price-support program would be $3 billion to $5 billion greater than in the absence of the ARP. Hence, while aimed at both supply control and budget discipline, it is the latter objective rather than the former that ARPs most successfully address.

The second agricultural policy objective, conservation of marginal agricultural lands, was to be achieved by the CRP. Under the CRP, landowners agree not to produce on highly erodible cropland[2] for 10 years

---

[1]The farm bill provides three instruments to control supply—acreage limitations, set-asides, and required diversions. All three, often used interchangeably in the literature, require that the farmer not plant some cropland in exchange for government subsidies. A "set-aside program" would require that the farmer not plant a particular proportion of "planted acres." An "acreage limitation program" would require that the farmer not plant a particular proportion of the "crop acreage base." "Required diversions" are additional to the other two and might be tied either to base or to planted acres. For 1986, USDA implemented an acreage limitation program with a small required diversion tied to base. A voluntary land diversion element was added for 1987. The distinctions are important to the extent that the base—the average of several years of planted and considered-planted acres—differs from planted acres, which is a one-year record only. All three supply-control mechanisms are subsumed under the rubric "acreage reduction program" here.

[2]At the time of writing, CRP eligibility was restricted to those croplands in Soil Conservation Service land capability classes VI-VIII, or currently cropped classes II-V lands that are eroding at more than three times the SCS-determined tolerance rate (3T or greater). There are an estimated 60 to 70 million acres of such land nationwide, 45 million acres of which are mandated by legislation to be retired over a five-year period. In 1987, the eligibility criterion was changed to cropland that has an erosion index (RKLS ÷ T) of 8 or greater and that is eroding at a rate higher than its T value.

in exchange for an annual CRP rental payment. Farmers submit sealed bids to USDA, indicating the acreage and the amount per acre they would be willing to accept annually in compensation for retiring the land. USDA then announces the maximum accepted bid level for the multicounty pool in which the farm is located. All acres bid at that rate or lower in the pool are enrolled in the CRP.

An axiom in economic policy analysis holds that for each policy objective there should be at least one instrument, and each instrument should be carefully designed to have maximum impact on its primary objective (8). The ARP violates this axiom insofar as it attempts to accomplish both supply control and budget discipline, with a little conservation thrown in as well. The CRP is also a single instrument with more than one objective. Conservation and supply control are built in, while budget discipline is implicit in the bid procedure. As with the ARP, the fact that a single instrument is intended to meet multiple objectives raises immediate questions of feasibility. None of the objectives may be met. There is already evidence that the CRP is failing to retire as much marginal land as it could, that it does not accomplish a great deal of supply control, and that bids are much higher than anticipated, thus frustrating the third agricultural policy objective—budget discipline.

The CRP is in trouble because of the lack of a clear match between instruments and objectives and because of two "program externalities" stemming from the concurrent operation of the CRP and price support programs. These are the "crowding out" and "base bite" effects. Both externalities raise the costs and reduce the effectiveness of the CRP.

These externalities can be illustrated from the farmer's perspective. First, consider the crowding out effect. Suppose that a farmer signed up for the price support program, which requires a one-year corn acreage reduction of 20 percent of corn base. A farmer with 120 acres of cropland and 90 acres of assigned corn base could plant 72 (90 x .80) acres to corn. The farmer must idle 18 acres to receive deficiency and other program payments calculated on the historic yield from 72 acres of permitted corn plantings.[3]

---

[3]Note that *any* 72 of the 120 acres of cropland on the farm could be planted to corn and *any* 18 could be idled. Program participants are paid the difference between a crop's target price and the actual price (or loan rate, if higher). A farm's official crop acreage base is an accounting entity used by the Agricultural Stabilization and Conservation Service to determine the magnitude of the deficiency payments for that commodity, based on historic planting records. The base is *not* a geographical designation. Hence, a particular acre should not be thought of as a "base acre" or a "nonbase acre." Deficiency payments are calculated for output "grown" on the farm's established base at the established yield. The farmer can plant no more of a program crop than the established base in that crop, less any ARP, although a farm may have bases for more than one crop.

Under these circumstances, it is in the farmer's interest to idle the most marginal acres first because these acres are least productive. Consequently, the ARP's potential impact on commodity supply is reduced. This "slippage" occurs because total farm income is derived from a combination of government payments *and* crop marketings. The more bushels that can be produced on the acres actually planted, the higher farm revenues will be. Indeed, in the past many farmers have been inclined to bring marginal acres into production just so that they will be available to set aside at some later date (*1, 2, 4*).

The important consequence of this slippage is that many CRP-eligible acres are idled under the ARP before they are even considered for the CRP. This "crowds out" eligible acres that might otherwise have entered the CRP; it effectively lowers the pool of eligible acres for the conservation reserve and raises the bids received for CRP entry. Slippage thus not only frustrates supply control, but, through the crowding out effect, frustrates conservation objectives as well.

The second program externality, the "base bite effect," is not unintended; it was designed to give the CRP a supply-control impact. For each acre entered into the reserve, the aggregate farm acreage base is reduced proportionately for the 10 years of the contract. A 120-acre farm with a 90-acre corn base will have its base reduced by 1/120, or .75 acre, for each acre entered into the CRP. A 10-acre CRP entry would reduce our farmer's assigned corn base from 90 to 82.5; this new base would then be subject to the 20 percent ARP, resulting in total permitted corn plantings of 66 acres.

The result of CRP participation, whether or not marginal ARP acres are actually designated first, is that an additional 6 acres (72-66) of corn land must be idled. This effect, which is distinct from the crowding out effect, we call the "base bite." If the 6 additional corn acres to be idled are more productive than those that would be idled under the ARP alone, the opportunity cost of removing them from production will also be higher and so will CRP bids. In fact, from the farmer's perspective the one-year marginal opportunity cost of additional CRP entry is the income foregone from the most productive acres idled under *either* program. The fact that the CRP is a 10-year contract makes putting productive acres into it even less attractive, further lowering the prospect that they will be retired at any but a high bid price.

The ironic and troubling result of these program interactions is that ARPs fail to control supply due to slippage, which, in turn, causes the CRP to lose eligible acres due to the crowding out effect. In addition, the base bite effect raises the opportunity cost of CRP participation and thus CRP bids. These conflicts frustrate both supply control and conservation objectives at the same time that they make both programs less cost-effective. The evidence from the first three rounds of CRP bidding supports this argument.

The CRP experience to date. Congress required that 5 million acres be enrolled in the CRP in 1986 and that an additional 40 million acres be added over the succeeding four years. USDA estimated that annual per acre CRP rental costs (exclusive of cover-crop establishment) would average $38 to $44 (6). To meet the 5-million-acre goal in 1986, USDA allocated $190 million. When the 1986 bids were examined, however, most were well above initial estimates. Agriculture Secretary Richard Lyng declared the bulk of them "unreasonable" and authorized payment for only 838,000 acres, at an average bid of $41. (Final contracts were signed on 754,000 acres). Enrollments were far from uniformly distributed across states—Minnesota and Colorado alone accounted for 21 percent of first-round CRP acreage. Table 1 shows first-round CRP experiences for Minnesota and the nation. The average bid is for those bids that fell under the maximum accepted bid in each pool. These were close to the initial USDA estimates, because the administration chose to keep program outlays "reasonable" by imposing a bid cap. This was accomplished at the expense of a great shortfall in terms of enrolled acreage, however.

The 1986 CRP enrollment period was subsequently reopened and at the same time early 1987 enrollments were accepted. This second round was much more successful in attracting bids at what USDA considered to be reasonable levels. Nationally, an additional 3 million acres were added; in Minnesota an additional 215,000 acres were added. (These totals were reported by USDA as 1986 CRP enrollments. Strictly speaking, however, they include a great many acres that will not be idled until the 1987 crop year.) The new CRP bids were still substantially above initial USDA estimates, however, now due not only to the program externalities but also

Table 1. First-round final CRP contracts: United States and Minnesota.

	Enrollment (1,000 acres)	Average Cost Per Acre ($)
Minnesota	65	48.09
United States	754	42.06

to the learning behavior of farmers in the first rounds. Evidently reflecting the thinking that USDA would stick to its relatively low first-round maximum accepted bid, the distributions of tendered bids narrowed considerably. Many more bids were accepted, but there were fewer bids made at the very low end. Consequently, weighed average accepted bids increased. Table 2 shows the experience to date in Minnesota pools 1 and 8.

Pool 1 is a wheat region, and pool 8 is a corn-soybean region. The simple average bid tendered and the maximum accepted bid are shown for comparison. By limiting accepted bids to those essentially at or below prevailing cash rental rates, USDA denied CRP participation to the bulk of interested landowners. High bids should have come as no surprise, however, given the program externalities discussed above and the fact that local cash rental rates historically fail to reflect farmers' expected incomes from land, particularly in periods of lucrative price support programs.

Revised targeting criteria. In general, the more attractive the price support program, the more expensive it is for the government to acquire CRP land. This is due both to the crowding out effect, which reduces the supply of CRP-eligible land and forces any CRP acreage onto more productive and more costly land, and to the base bite effect, which shifts the relevant foregone income calculation from the CRP acre to the highest valued land removed from production. If the base bite provision were removed from the CRP legislation, then the individual CRP bids could be determined strictly on the basis of the marginal productivity of alternate crops.

Table 2. Distributions for first two CRP bidding rounds: Minnesota pools 1 and 8.

| | Round | | |
| | | 2 | |
	1	1986	1987
Pool 1:			
Mean bid tendered	52.44	42.79	44.40
Standard deviation bid tendered	19.74	8.79	7.83
Maximum bid accepted	44.00	44.00	44.00
Mean bid accepted	36.27	39.93	40.54
Pool 8:			
Mean bid tendered	101.14	82.62	86.65
Standard deviation bid tendered	46.53	17.50	17.48
Maximum bid accepted	85.00	85.00	85.00
Mean bid accepted	69.95	77.18	80.08

Direct competition with the price-support program would vanish, and total CRP acreage would increase within a budget constraint. To remove the pernicious effects of the crowding out and base bite externalities, one or both programs must be revised to exclude from eligibility those lands targeted for the other program. Here we present a targeting scheme to accomplish this reform.

The two program externalities can be eliminated if each program is targeted to maximize its impact upon a single objective—supply control in the case of the ARP and marginal land conservation in the case of the CRP. Such a targeting scheme should employ two basic criteria for the land in question: (1) its inherent agricultural productivity and (2) its inherent capacity to resist soil erosion. Both are quantifiable using data on crop yields and measures of soil erodibility. A variety of such measures are possible, and no specific measure need be used in every case. All are designed to overcome the administrative rigidity and subjective qualities associated with the now-traditional use of soil erosion tolerance levels (T values) in policymaking. For illustration, we here employ the "productivity index" and "resistivity index" developed at the University of Minnesota (7). The productivity index (PI) indexes soil according to its suitability as an environment for plant roots; it is based on available water capacity, bulk density, and pH. The index ranges from 0.0 to 1.0, where 1.0 is associated with that soil (within a given area of analysis) that has the best rooting environment. The resistivity index (RI) is a measure of a soil's vulnerability to erosion; it is based on topographic factors (RKLS)[4] from the universal soil loss equation and on the degree of potential loss of favorable rooting zone as the soil is eroded. Wind erosion is accommodated by incorporating factors (ICL)[5] from the wind erosion equation. All soils are ranked on a 0.0 to 1.0 scale, with 1.0 assigned to soils extremely resistant to erosion-caused losses in production.

Together, PI and RI allow any geographic area (farm, township, county, state) to be ranked on the basis of its soils' inherent productivity and resistivity characteristics. Land parcels (or soil classes) can be thought of as falling into one of four subsets, according to each parcel's position along the PI and RI gradients (Figure 1).[6] This categorization permits us to apply particular policy instruments to each of the three agricultural policy objectives—supply control, conservation of marginal agricultural lands, and budget discipline. We argue that the appropriate instruments to achieve

[4]R = rainfall and runoff; K = soil erodibility; L = slope length; S = slope steepness.
[5]I = soil erodibility; C = climatic factor; L = unsheltered distance.

each of the policy objectives are, respectively, (1) the ARP, (2) the CRP, and (3) a land classification scheme designating productivity and resistivity criteria for program coverage. This matching permits a fully identified set of three policy instruments with three policy objectives.

The logic underlying the targeting of these instruments is straightforward. Soils that are resistant to erosion and highly productive (RP) are precisely those on which production should be encouraged. It is on these that the long-run comparative advantage of the United States lies as an exporter and low-cost producer. On less resistant but still productive soils, erosion damage must be compensated for by using more costly practices and higher levels of inputs. Lands that are both resistant to erosion damage and nonproductive (RNP) are inappropriate as targets for either supply control or soil conservation, unless they have special features (such as rare wildlife or habitat), in which case a separate objective, such as protected habitat, is appropriate. A strong argument can be made for the development of such additional objectives, especially concerning off-site effects of soil erosion (3, 5).

On soils that are nonresistant and productive (NRP), ARPs should first be applied. There are three reasons for this matching. First, because they are productive, idling of these soils will result in larger and more cost-effective supply reductions than would idling less productive soils, as is presently permitted. Slippage is thereby reduced. While ARPs on the resistant/productive soils may be justified in the name of supply control as well, it makes sense to begin idling the more vulnerable nonresistant/productive soils first, working into more resistant soils along the resistivity gradient

[6]The RI and PI indexes disentangle two components of the SCS land capability classification system.

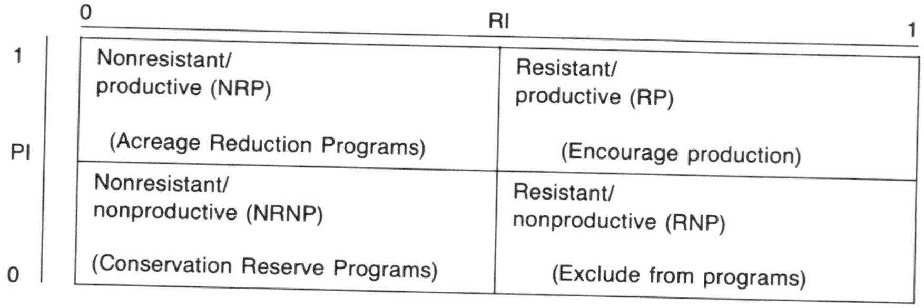

Figure 1. Locating soils in productivity/resistivity space.

only as surpluses become intolerable. The second reason to apply the ARP first on nonresistant/productive lands is that it is cheaper to idle these soils under the ARP than it would be to retire them under the CRP—simply because they are more productive and, hence, more costly. Overall market value increases as one moves up and to the right on the diagram. Budget discipline is more possible by the coercive power of the ARP than by the use of the voluntary CRP process. The third argument in favor of the ARP on nonresistant/productive soils, as opposed to nonresistant/nonproductive soils, is one of management flexibility. In contrast to the 10-year CRP contract, the 1-year ARP requirement allows supply control to ebb and flow on a yearly cycle in response to supply conditions, relaxing in times of relative shortfall and increasing in times of surplus. In particular, in the event of national or international emergencies, it may be justifiable to crop previously idled, nonresistant but productive soils.

Lands that are nonresistant and nonproductive (NRNP) are those lands on which the CRP should concentrate. Because they are relatively unproductive but highly vulnerable to erosion, their retirement will be the most cost-effective way to maximize soil conservation for a given amount of retired acreage without reducing the amount of productive lands under cultivation. Also, precisely because they are unproductive, they will cost less to bring into the CRP.

A proposal for legislative reform

The land targeting scheme outlined in the previous section provides a basis for three key reforms in the farm bill. These reforms would improve the capacity of the federal government to (a) control supply, (b) promote conservation, and (c) reduce the costs of current programs. Some of the necessary changes could be made administratively, without specific congressional authorization.

First, ARPs should be restricted to high productivity-low resistivity lands, and the CRP should focus on low productivity-low resistivity lands. If additional supply control is necessary, then ARPs could be extended on a year-to-year basis to more resistant soils, but only after all less resistant soils are set aside. One option would be to introduce a 3- to 5-year ARP for lands in the high productivity-low resistivity category, midway between the 10-year CRP and 1-year ARPs on more resistant soils. Such a scheme is outlined by Berner (1).

Second, those lands eligible for the CRP should be declared *ineligible* for the ARP. The converse, however, would not hold. More productive land with low resistivity could still be entered into the 10-year CRP. By decoupling program eligibility in this manner, the crowding out effect would be eliminated, thereby raising the pool of eligible acres for the CRP, reducing CRP bids, and lowering overall program costs.

Third, current provisions attempting to make the CRP an instrument of supply control—the base bite—should be eliminated. Enrollment in the CRP should not be tied to reductions in farm acreage base.

All three proposals would lower the cost of the CRP and let ARPs more effectively control supply. Contrast this approach[7] and the status quo, in which slippage brings unproductive soils into the ARP, frustrating supply control and, by the crowding out effect, forcing the CRP to pick up more productive and more costly acres, acres made even more expensive by the base bite. With ARPs targeted directly to productive land, the CRP could be left to focus on its primary objective: conservation.

[7]The particular definition of productivity and resistivity need not be confined to the indexes used in Minnesota, nor to any given level of these criteria. Given a particular set of supply control, conservation, and budget goals, the level at which PI and RI are "cut" to determine program coverage is flexible. In Minnesota, for example, a state conservation reserve program has been developed that makes eligible only those lands located among the lowest 25 percent of each gradient. (The Minnesota program also sets state payments at 90 percent of the average accepted CRP bid to avoid state revenues being spent when federal revenues would otherwise be committed.) As another example, a CRP might be designed for low RI but mid-range PI lands on the supposition that market forces will automatically retire the lowest PI lands on their own.

REFERENCES

1. Berner, Alfred H. 1984. *Federal land retirement program: A land management albatross.* In *Transactions of the Forty-ninth North American Wildlife and Natural Resources Conference.* Wildlife Management Institute, Washington, D.C.
2. Christensen, Raymond P., and Ronald O. Aines. 1962. *Economic effects of acreage control programs in the 1950s.* Agricultural Economic Report No. 18. Economic Research Service, U.S. Department of Agriculture, Washington, D.C.
3. Crosson, P. R., and A. T. Stout. 1983. *Productivity effects of U.S. cropland erosion.* Resources for the Future, Washington, D.C.
4. Heimlich, Ralph E. 1986. *Agricultural programs and cropland conversion.* Land Economics 62(2): 174-181.
5. McSweeny, William T., and Randall A. Kramer. 1986. *Farm programs for achieving soil conservation and nonpoint pollution control.* Land Economics 62(2): 159-173.
6. Ogg, Clayton, W., Shwu-Eng Webb, and Wen-Yuan Huang. 1984. *Cropland acreage reduction alternatives: An economic analysis of a soil conservation reserve and competitive bids.* Journal of Soil and Water Conservation 39(6): 379-383.
7. Runge, C. F., W. E. Larson, and G. Roloff. 1986. *Using productivity measures to target conservation program: A comparative analysis.* Journal of Soil and Water Conservation 41(1): 45-49.

8. Tinbergen, Ian. 1952. *On the theory of economic policy.* Elvesier-North Holland, The Netherlands.

2

Complexity of the landscape[1]

Francis J. Pierce

The theme of this book, "Making Soil and Water Conservation Work," suggests that the task of soil and water conservation is far from complete and perhaps is jeopardized by scientific as well as state and federal policy perspectives. Possibly, as Lovejoy and Napier suggest (11), technology is a necessary condition for conserving soil but not a sufficient condition. Government policies, program implementation, and human behavior may be as important as technology. Perhaps conservation technology is inadequate to meet the challenge of today's agriculture because it is in conflict with modern production technology. Are existing limitations of soil and water conservation technology, such as crop limitations of conservation tillage, insurmountable, or has research been focused away from development of appropriate technologies? Or is the technology sufficient and public policies on soil and water conservation inappropriate? Perhaps, as Batie suggests (2), the traditional view, wherein a farmer has the right to allow the land to erode and conservation is considered a production system input, should give way to an alternative perspective that does not take a protective stance toward the status quo and in which the farmer is no longer perceived as the steward of the environment. Perhaps all interested in making soil and water conservation work have failed to comprehend fully the complexity of soils in the landscape.

The proper context for the discussion of policy on soil and water quality should center on the soil as a three-dimensional body having spatial

[1] Michigan Agriculture Experiment Station Journal Number 12265.

patterns and occupying landscape positions. From the scientific perspective, the degree of success in efforts to make soil and water conservation work will be determined by how well we understand the soil-landscape relationships and focus on them with our research, public policies, and programs.

The problem

Hugh Hammond Bennett presented a comprehensive statement on the science and practice of soil conservation in his book *Soil Conservation* (*3*). Subsequent writings by many have articulated the various aspects of soil and water conservation, updating the great wealth of knowledge now available. More recently, the 1977 and 1982 National Resources Inventories provided the best quantitative estimates to date of the magnitude and areal distribution of soil erosion from wind and water in the United States. Analysis of these inventories has shown the following:

▶ Soil erosion remains a major problem in the United States.

▶ The erosion problem is unevenly distributed, being concentrated on a small percentage of the cropland acres in the United States.

▶ Wind erosion may be a substantial problem in humid regions, for example, Michigan and Minnesota. Estimates of wind erosion had been limited to the Great Plains prior to the 1982 NRI.

▶ Present technology is inadequate to quantify properly the soil erosion problem, especially wind erosion (*9*) and concentrated flow erosion (*7*), as well as the off-site movement of eroded soil (*4*).

▶ The primary focus of science and public policy has shifted toward off-site concerns and away from the traditional concern about degradation of soil resources, primarily losses in soil productivity and the adequacy of the resource base for future food and fiber production.

The shift toward off-site concerns especially illustrates how science and resource information can directly influence soil and water conservation policy. The change in focus from on-site productivity losses to off-site effects is attributable to a number of things operating in succession.

First, our understanding of the magnitude and extent of soil erosion in the United States is the best in history. This is a direct result of legislation mandating the 1977 and 1982 NRIs: Public Law 92-419, the Rural Development Act, passed by Congress in 1972.

Second, the resource data provided by the NRIs provided greater insight into the potential impacts of erosion on soil productivity. Analysis of the 1977 NRI data in the 1980 Resources Conservation Act appraisal gave early indications that the erosion-induced decline in soil productivity was less than anticipated from the presumed magnitude of the erosion problem and from impacts indicated by earlier erosion studies. A major Corn Belt study on the impact of soil erosion on long-term soil productivity estimated the reduction in productivity to be less than 8 percent in any major land resource area (*14, 16*). The large percentage of land in low slope classes combined with deep, fertile soils contributed to this result.

Crosson and Stout (*6*), after viewing the early results of the Corn Belt study, along with the analysis reported in the RCA and some of their own, concluded that on-site concerns about erosion may be over-emphasized and that off-site concerns, such as water quality, may be equally or more costly impacts of soil erosion. Their attention was then directed at other costs of erosion, resulting in quite revealing estimates about the real costs of off-site movement of runoff water and associated sediments.

Estimates by Clark and colleagues (*5*) have confirmed that off-site costs of erosion far exceed earlier estimates and may be many times the on-site costs (*5*).

Finally, the need to improve technology to better quantify erosion processes occuring on the landscape level, especially concentrated flow erosion, was recognized in the shift in focus to off-site concerns. To a large extent, this involves the use of remote sensing and graphic-information-system technologies, along with more sophisticated process-level erosion models.

While the focus of efforts may be more encompassing today, the problem remains one of putting soil and water conservation practices on the land to secure sustained food production and a quality environment.

Soils and landscapes

Understanding soils and their interrelationships within a landscape is requisite to making soil and water conservation work. As indicated earlier, it is often the misunderstanding of soils and landscapes that inhibits progress in soil and water conservation.

Scale is an important factor in this discussion because it reveals a great deal about science and state and federal policy on soil and water conservation. The erosion problem manifests itself quite differently as one addresses it from the broad scale of the world view, national view, the state and local view, and finally through the very basic view of the research soil scientist.

Table 1 illustrates the relationship among scale, soils, and landscapes and the scope of soil and water conservation activities. For discussion purposes, set the scale from microns to land resource regions in the United States. The viewpoint spans that from the basic research scientist to the policymaker in Congress. The scope ranges from fundamental soil properties and processes to national soil and water policy. The problem is soil and water conservation. The context is soil as an integral part of the landscape.

Basic research in soil science often deals with soils as collections of materials; the scale is in microns to centimeters. At this scale, scientists pursue knowledge about fundamental properties and processes in soil, such as clay type and amount, soil detachment, soil structure, soil fertility, and organic matter dynamics. The resolution at this scale is much too fine for

Table 1. The scale of soils and landscapes relative to the scope of soil and water conservation.

Scale	Soils and Landscapes	Scope
Microns to centimeters	Soils as collections of materials	Soil detachment, fertility, organic matter Soil characterization
Meters	Soil profile Pedon	Soil Classification, soil productivity
Cubic meters	Soil body Soil series Polypedons	Capabilities and limitations
Hectares	Soil mapping units, soil associations	Soil survey, USLE, WEQ, NRI
Kilometers	Landscapes	Water quality, concentrated flow, Crop production (farmer), policy implementation
Major Land Resource Areas	Soil regions	RCA appraisal, state and federal planning
Land resource regions	National soil resources	Regional and national planning

those concerned with soil and water conservation policy, but basic information at this level is key to understanding the problems and solutions of soil and water conservation.

The soil profile becomes clear as the scale increases to meters. The concept of soil profile lends itself to understanding the various dimensions of soils. Soils are classified according to the presence or absence of horizons in the soil profile and the degree of soil development in each. Productivity analyses operate at this level of resolution, viewing soil productivity as the potential productive capacity in the context of the soil profile. The scope at this scale is soil characterization.

Soil is more correctly defined as a three-dimensional body. Here, the scale is in the range of cubic meters, and shape, slope, and spacial variability are active considerations. Multiple soil bodies having the same range of characteristics form the concept of the soil series. Certain capabilities and limitations of soils are determined at this scale.

Soils form an association with other soils in a complex arrangement in the landscape. The soil scientist uses the soil-landscape relationships to map soils. The soil mapping unit is the basis of the cooperative soil survey. The scale is hectares, and the scope is soil mapping units, resource inventories, and point estimates of erosion, as with the universal soil loss equation (USLE) and wind erosion equation (WEQ).

As the scale broadens to many hectares and kilometers, soils on the landscape, or soilscapes, become the predominant unit. Soil mapping units occur in the landscape, which are themselves a collection of landforms. Soil surveys, water quality, concentrated flow erosion, land capability classification, and most important, crop production operate at this scale. The relationship of crop production to the soilscape directly influences soil and water conservation because the implementation of policy occurs at this level.

State and federal policy perspectives are concerned with attaining certain soil and water conservation ideals rather than protecting specific parcels of land (18). Policy traditionally attempts to influence land use through cost-sharing and other incentive programs (or more recently through disincentives, as in the case of conservation compliance). The policy has long recognized regional differences in soils, landscapes, and climatic zones and their impacts on crop production and land use. The need for a broader perspective mandates that policy often operate at a regional scale. Policy implementation, however, occurs at the scale of the farmer or land user. Therefore, federal and state policy must strive for the ideal in recognition of regional differences. Policy implementation must be designed to reflect the soil in the landscape.

It is clear that to make soil and water conservation work, the scientist must broaden and the policymakers must focus their perspectives to the scale of the soil of the landscape. The implementation of programs on a watershed basis is a move in that direction. The technology needed to facilitate this is on the horizon in the form of remote sensing, geographic information systems (GIS), and improved resource data bases provided, for example, by the progression of the National Cooperative Soil Survey.

Complexity of the landscape

The character of the landscape dictates the spatial arrangement of soils and water features. These together with climate determine to a large extent the erosion processes and potential soil and water problems. Figure 1a illustrates the major soil delineations for a typical landscape in Indiana as they might appear in a county soil survey (8). While useful for understanding the areal extent and spatial distribution of soils, the soil delineation is less informative, in itself, about erosion potential as it relates to off-site movement of sediments. The three-dimensional landscape view in figure 1b illustrates the dramatic difference in perception afforded by the landscape view of soils compared with a planar view (8). In this diagram it is very evident where sheet and rill erosion, concentrated flow erosion, and sediment deposition will occur, but not so clear where wind erosion will be a factor. Crystal clear in figure 1b is the importance of understanding the complex relationships between soils and erosion processes within the landscape.

The complexity of the landscape is relatively easy to illustrate. Its importance to soil and water conservation is best illustrated by the following examples.

Soil productivity and erosion process relationships

There are many aspects of landscapes that affect soil productivity and erosion. Consider a common landscape in south central Minnesota. The soil association includes the Storden, Clarion, Nicollet, Webster, and Glencoe soil series. The soils were formed in loamy glacial till under a natural vegetation of tall-grass prairie. The Storden soil is well drained and occupies the upland position in the landscape; the Glencoe soil is in the lowest position, occupying drainageways and depressions (Figure 2). The relationship among the soils is shown in Figure 3 (13). For each soil, the figure

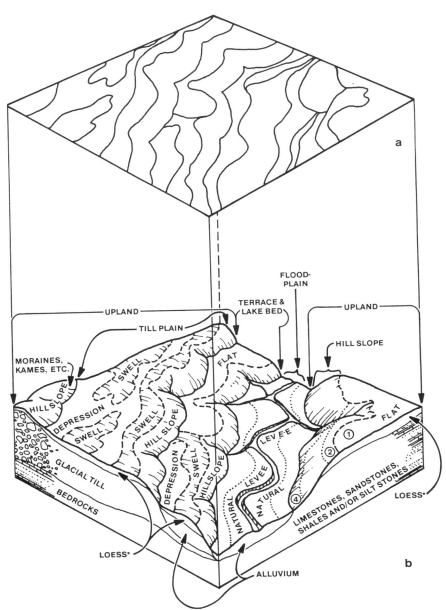

Figure 1. Illustration of the complexity of landscapes relative to soil mapping units.

lists productivity, as indicated by a productivity index (PI) and average corn yield, along with drainage class. Erosion moves sediment from the Storden, Clarion, and Nicollet soil areas to areas of deposition within the Webster and Glencoe soil areas. Productivity, as indicated by PI, increases from the erodible Storden soil to the depositional Glencoe soil. Corn yields follow the increase in PI until drainage becomes an additional factor limiting yield. The PI rates the suitability of the soil profile for crop growth but neglects the influence of inadequate drainage on yield.

Pierce and colleagues (14) evaluated soil productivity declines in the Corn Belt on the basis of changes in the soil profile characteristics that determine soil productivity. They estimated productivity losses of less than 8 percent for cropland acres in any major land resource area when the data were weighted by areal extent of soils. While on a regional basis these

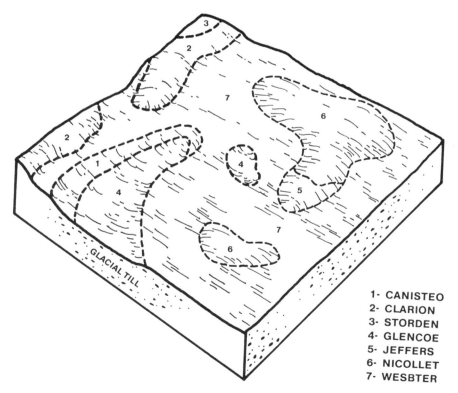

1- CANISTEO
2- CLARION
3- STORDEN
4- GLENCOE
5- JEFFERS
6- NICOLLET
7- WESBTER

Figure 2. Block diagram of soil associations in a closed watershed of south central Minnesota (10).

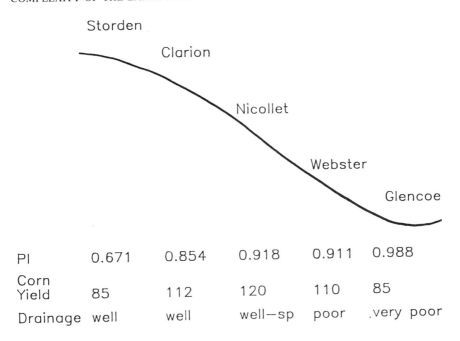

PI   0.671   0.854   0.918   0.911   0.988

Corn
Yield   85   112   120   110   85

Drainage   well   well   well—sp   poor   ,very poor

Soils were formed in a tall grass prairie in loamy glacial till.

Figure 3. Productivity relationships in a landscape of south central Minnesota (13).

estimates may reflect the true long-term productivity concerns about erosion, at least in the study area they do not reflect concerns about erosion from the perspective of soils in the landscape. Figure 4 shows the distribution of soil productivity losses by slope class for the cropland soils in the Corn Belt (*13*). Soil erosion increases with increasing slope class, as expected. Soil productivity losses also increase with slope class, but the pattern is different because of differences in the vulnerability of soils in the Corn Belt to erosion-induced productivity losses. While this pattern of increased productivity losses exists in the Corn Belt, the preponderance of cropland hectares in the lower slope classes diminishes the regional impact of long-term productivity losses. Put another way, if 25 percent of cropland acres had significant losses in 100 years, while 75 percent remained relatively stable, the regional impact may be inconsequential, but the local impact may be devastating. Hence, the case is made for a targeting approach to soil and water conservation.

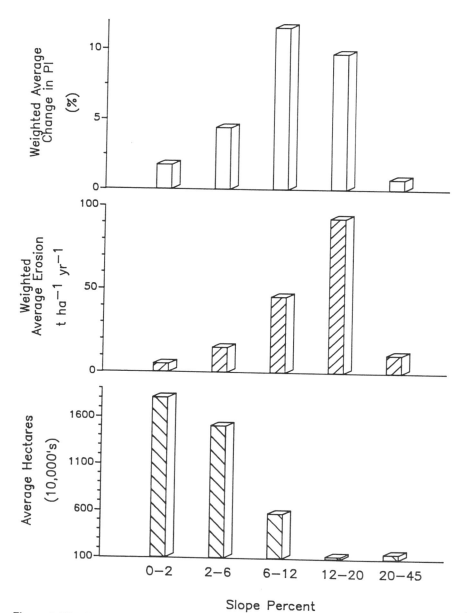

Figure 4. Distribution of average sheet and rill erosion rate, weighted average change in productivity index after 100 years of erosion, and hectares by slope class for cropland in the Corn Belt region of the United States (*13*).

The relationship of soils to the landscape is important to water quality. Movement of sediment from a cultivated area may affect long-term soil productivity either in the area of erosion or in the area of deposition. The extent to which sediment will contribute to water quality problems is a function of the character of the landscape. For example, figure 2 shows that sediment carried into the area of Glencoe soil may never leave the cultivated area. This may be the case with landscapes that have little relief, no major surface outlet, and containment of runoff water and sediment in depressional areas (10). In contrast, figure 5 illustrates a landscape characterized by distinct slopes and deep, incised streams. This landscape may contribute significant quantities of eroded sediment to adjacent water bodies (10). Concern about off-site damages by erosion must be guided by a thorough understanding of the soils in the landscape.

Onstad and associates (12) illustrated the impact of soil movement and deposition in the landscape. Figure 6a shows a loessial landscape in southeastern Minnesota. The predicted erosion and deposition on a natural transect of that landscape is given in figure 6b, and the impact of erosion on long-term productivity after 100 years is given in figure 6c. Soil erosion over many years will affect the soils, depending upon landscape posi-

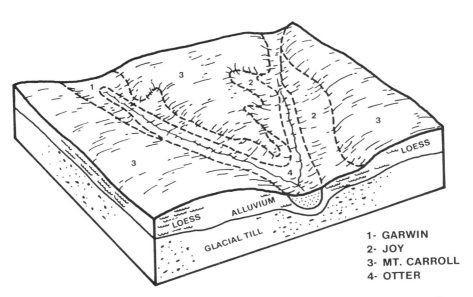

Figure 5. Block diagram of soil associations in an open watershed in southeastern Minnesota (10).

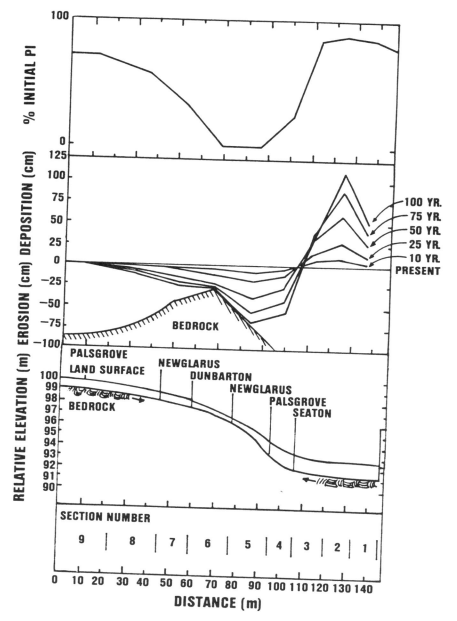

Figure 6. Erosion-productivity relationships in a landscape of southeastern Minnesota (12).

tion and soil profile characteristics. Erosion is most severe in the slope and upland positions and will result in reduced productivity. Deposition occurs at the toe of the landscape and may positively or negatively affect productivity. In erodible portions of the landscape, where bedrock is close to the soil surface, productivity will decline to zero as erosion depletes the soil. Where the soil and loess material are thick, soil productivity will decline, but more slowly. This analysis clearly shows (a) that a soil landscape should be the basic unit for determining productivity changes over time as a result of erosion and (b) that productivity changes indexed on soil mapping units may give misleading information about changes in productivity unless their positions in the landscape are considered (12). The importance of landscape in understanding soils and erosion processes is demonstrated well by these examples, and the implications for making soil and water conservation work must not be underestimated.

Targeting resources for effective conservation

As Batie suggests (2), while the proposition for targeting is appealing, the criteria for it are not quite clear. The technology upon which to establish such criteria is precisely the role of the scientific community.

The debate over which criteria are most suitable for targeting federal dollars has been lively. The Congress passed important conservation legislation in the 1985 farm bill, which represents a big step in targeting federal dollars to erodible land. The criteria selected for targeting were based on the land capability classification system long used by the Soil Conservation Service. This has been deemed inappropriate by many who support a system based on the ratio of the potential for erosion to T, the maximum tolerable annual soil loss (4). This criterion is widely praised but the concept of the T value is itself a subject of considerable controversy. New criteria, proposed by Runge and associates (17), are based on concepts of productivity, vulnerability, and erosion potential presented by Pierce and colleagues (14). In this scheme (Figure 7), soils are rated according to their productivity (PI) and their vulnerability to erosion (RI). RI is a resistivity index based on the potential for wind and water erosion. Targeting priority would be to protect productive, nonresistant soils first, to the exclusion of soils more resistant to erosion. Taff and Runge (19) have proposed extending this concept to improve the effectiveness of the Conservation Reserve Program and the Acreage Reduction Program authorized in the 1985 farm bill.

These criteria are an improvement over alternatives in that they consider quantitatively both erosion potential and soil productivity. They suffer, however, like the other proposed criteria in failing to consider off-site erosion concerns, especially those related to water quality. This third dimension of the soil and water conservation problem is critical since off-site concerns of water quality may exceed those of on-site concerns as discussed earlier.

Consider the following scheme. Soils may occupy landscape positions that have a range of potential to contribute sediment to a water body. They also vary in the quantity of sediment that they can contribute, based on their erosion potential. Therefore, soils and landscapes can be characterized by their potential to contribute sediment to a water body and by their potential to move sediment from the local area, in addition to their erosion potential. These potentials can be combined to form a nonpoint-source index, NPSI. A low NPSI would be assigned to soils that occupy landscape positions where the potential for sediment delivery is low or where sediment is unlikely to leave the landscape. A high NPSI would be assigned to soils in landscapes with high potential for delivery to a water body.

Now apply this concept to the PI-RI scheme, as illustrated in figure 8. If the catagories proposed by Taff and Runge (*19*) are expanded to include the nonpoint-source pollution dimension, eight catagories emerge

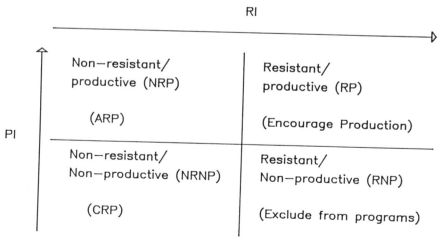

Figure 7. Scheme for targeting government programs based on productivity (PI) and resistivity (RI) indices (*19*).

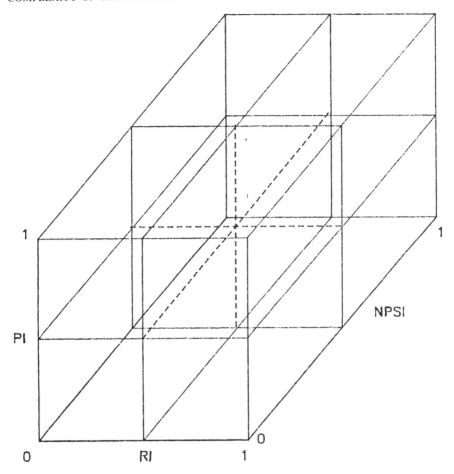

Figure 8. Illustration of a three-dimensional scheme for targeting government programs based on productivity (PI), resistivity (RI), and nonpoint-source pollution (NPSI) indices.

(Table 2). Productive land with resistance to and little potential for nonpoint-source pollution would be ineligible for both the ARP and CRP. This would also be the case for resistant, nonproductive land with a low nonpoint-source pollution potential. The priority for ARP eligibility would be resistant, productive land with a high nonpoint-source potential or nonresistant, productive land with a low potential for nonpoint-source pollution. The priority for consideration in the case of the CRP would be nonresistant, productive land and nonproductive, nonresistant land with a high potential for nonpoint-source pollution. Other land eligible for inclusion in the CRP would be nonproductive, resistant land with a high potential for nonpoint-source pollution and nonproductive, nonresistant land with a low potential for nonpoint-source pollution.

This scheme is comprehensive in that it includes the three dimensions of the water quality problem: it identifies erodible land and quantitatively addresses both the soil and water quality dimensions. In addition, any measure of productivity, resistivity, and potential for nonpoint-source pollution would fit this targeting structure. One technology to use this structure is available (*14, 16, 17, 19*). The scheme proposed here overcomes criticisms of the NRIs in their applicability to water quality problems. It would be feasible to update the 1982 NRI to include observations that would in fact allow some regional targeting and quota estimation with existing data bases.

The adoption of conservation tillage

Many studies have addressed the adoption of conservation tillage, but in these studies there seems to have been little interest in the landscape relative to the adoption of conservation tillage. Perhaps more insight into the adoption process might be gained by including the aspects of the landscape as a factor in such analyses.

Clearly, conservation tillage has not been applied on the most erodible land (*15*). In fact, the adoption of conservation practices in general has

Table 2. Categories for targeting soil and water conservation resources based on soil productivity, resistivity to erosion, and potential for nonpoint-source pollution.

Class*			
Productivity Index	Resistivity Index	Nonpoint-Source Pollution Index	Program eligiblity†
P	R	Low	None [prime farmland]
		High	Priority ARP
	NR	Low	Priority ARP
		High	Priority CRP
NP	R	Low	None
		High	CRP
	NR	Low	CRP
		High	Priority CRP

*P = productive, NP = nonproductive, R = resistant, NR = non-resistant.
†ARP = Areage Reduction Program, CRP = Conservation Reserve Program. The omission of the modifier "priority" indicates less emphasis for the intended program.

Table 3. Adoption of conservation practices on cropland in the United States.

Erosion Potential RKLS (ton/acres)	Cropland (million/acres)	Percent	Land Treated with One or More Conservation Practices (million/acres)	%
0<10	220	52	129	58
10<20	93	22	49	53
20<40	55	13	27	50
40<60	20	5	9	47
60<100	17	4	8	47
100<150	8	2	4	47
≥150	7	2	4	47

been unaffected by potential for erosion (Table 3). In some MLRAs, such as MLRA 103, most of the land in conservation tillage has low potential for water erosion (Table 4). In others, such as MLRAs 105 and 136, considered critically eroding areas by the Soil Conservation Service, most of the land in conservation tillage was erodible. Conservation tillage adoption in other areas, like MLRA 134, was intermediate.

If land needing conservation practices were actually receiving it, one would expect the plot of the C factor in the USLE versus potential erosion (RKLS product) to have a negative slope. Nationally, the trend showed no substantive change in C factor with increasing erosion potential, indicating the failure of conservation practices to be applied on erodible land (Figure 9). Perhaps less attention should be paid to acceptance rates of conservation practices and more to the soils and landscapes where these practices have been applied.

Land use relations and soils and landscapes

A particular use of a parcel of land is determined by a large number of interacting factors. The best use of land is determined by climate, productive capacity of soil, farm structure (e.g., animals versus cash crop), market considerations, availability of resources (e.g., water), available technology, competing uses, land tenure, farmer skill, perceived soil constraints, and the landscape. Perhaps land use is less and less a result of natural factors and more and more a matter of assembling cost-effective technologies (1).

For this discussion, the question may well be rephrased as follows: How do soil and landscape dictate land use, and what is the impact on soil and water conservation? Consider the following situations.

The P factor in the USLE is a measure of the effectiveness of conservation measures, such as terracing, stripcropping, and contour farming, in reducing sheet and rill erosion. While important in erosion control and in many parts of the country, the P factor in Michigan averaged 1.0 for all cropland in the 1982 NRI, indicating these conservation practices are not used in this state. The reason is simple. These traditional conservation practices commonly do not fit the complex landscapes in Michigan.

A common practice for dairy and cattle farmers is to graze their animals in the floodplains of streams and rivers because these areas are unsuited to managed crop production. Grazing of this land has long been recommended by agronomists as a good use. Recently, however, agriculture has become more aware of its contribution to nonpoint-source pollution, and use of this particular land for grazing is now recognized as incompatible with water quality goals. Yet, there is likely not a dairy region in the United States that could claim this is not a common use for this land. This example serves to demonstrate how concepts of best land use are changing in response to environmental concerns.

Over the years, sufficient examples have illuminated the incompatability of government policies and programs with respect to best land use. As an example, consider the ARP for 1986. This program required a farmer to idle land in exchange for government price supports. When restrictions on the idled land are relaxed and the farmer is allowed to put the set-aside land into production, the farmer must confront and solve weedy problems in his field before many of the weeds go to seed. The least expensive and most common solution is plowing, often leaving the land dormant until spring planting. But this solution creates a new, though obvious, problem—land that may be erodible is made vulnerable to erosion for an extended period. Government programs, therefore, need to consider landscape characteristics when planning and implementing public policies and pro-

Table 4. Distribution of conservation tillage by potential for erosion in four major land resource areas in the United States (15).

MLRA	Cropland (million/acres)	Conservation Tillage (% acres)	Land in Conservation Tillage by Erosion Class (RKLS;tons/acre/year)		
			< 10	10-20	> 20
			%		
103	14.4	13	65	20	16
105	8.8	23	7	12	80
134	7.5	14	2	41	63
136	4.2	12	6	14	81

NATIONAL SUMMARY

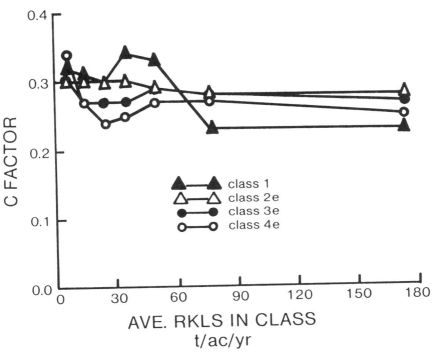

Figure 9. Plot of C-factor versus potential for erosion (RKLS) for four land capability subclasses for cropland in the United States (15).

grams that affect soil and water conservation.

The solution to insuring better use of land is, in part, found in the improvement of the technology and content of resource information and its communication to policymakers. Remote sensing and geographic-information-system technology will play an important role in the future. Certainly, policymakers must be exposed to the technology and resource information now available and provide for the development of the technology needed in the future to make soil and water conservation work.

Inventory of resources

When the subject of resource inventories arises, three important activities come to mind. The first is the national cooperative soil survey, which is paramount to a successful soil resource information base that will serve us well into the twenty-first century. Associated with this is the development of geographic information systems to integrate soil survey with other resource information.

The second activity consists of resource inventories, such as the 1977 and 1982 NRIs. Remote sensing technology will play an important role in enhancing our knowledge about uses of natural resources as they change in time. This role will include an ability to document changing land use and the impact of policy on the effectiveness of soil and water conservation.

The third activity is the development and improvement of models designed to use the information obtained through the soil survey and resource inventories. These models will allow us to project the impacts of land use and to assess and test the impacts of public policies on the quantity and quality of the soil and water resource base in the United States. The use of models and resource data already has allowed the indentification of critical areas where constraints to land use or threats to water quality exist; this use has also allowed the quantification of erosion impacts. Future refinements will even further improve these assessments.

Perhaps a weak link in resource information is the extent of soil characterization data needed as input for models and supporting data for resource information collected through the soil survey or remote sensing. Some soil characterization data are available, but more quantitative data are needed. Very specific and controlled sampling programs should be initiated soon to upgrade the soil data base in the United States to support revisions of and replacements for the USLE and WEQ. Consideration should also be given to the benefits of updating the 1982 NRI to improve its capacity to estimate water quality concerns of soil erosion.

Conclusions

Making soil and water conservation work has proven difficult for many reasons—some technical, some socioeconomic, some political. Soils and how and where they occur in the landscape provide the context in which to discuss the problem. The complex relationships of soils and water within the landscape are the basis for the erosion problem, and their understanding forms the basis for its solution. All dimensions of the soil and water conservation effort, from science to public policy, will better serve that cause if the context is always the soil and its position in the landscape.

Our understanding of the complexity of the landscape and its importance to soil and water conservation is improving as the nation progresses with the cooperative soil survey and the development of geographic information systems and remote sensing technologies. Significant progress already has been made through the use and analysis of the NRIs. While the challenge of soil and water conservation remains, the technology of tomorrow is near at hand.

REFERENCES

1. Avery, D. 1985. *Agriculture in the next 20 years.* In *1985 Yearbook of Agriculture.* U.S. Department of Agriculture, Washington, D.C.
2. Batie, S. 1986. *Why soil erosion: A social science perspective.* In S. B. Lovejoy and T. L. Napier [editors] *Conserving Soil: Insights from Socioeconomic Research,* Soil Conservation Society of America, Ankeny, Iowa.
3. Bennett, H. H. 1939. *Soil conservation.* McGraw-Hill, New York, New York.
4. Board of Agriculture, National Research Council. 1986. *Soil conservation: Assessing the National Resources Inventory, Volume 1.* National Academy Press, Washington, D.C. 314 pp.
5. Clark, E. H. II, J. A. Haverkamp, and W. Chapman. 1985. *Eroding soils: Off-farm impacts.* The Conservation Foundation, Washington, D.C.
6. Crosson, P. R., and T. Stout. 1983. *Productivity effects of cropland erosion in the United States.* Resources for the Future, Washington, D.C.
7. Foster, G. R. 1986. *Understanding ephemeral gully erosion.* In *Soil Conservation: Assessing the National Resources Inventory, Volume 2.* National Academy Press, Washington, D.C. pp. 90-124.
8. Galloway, H. M., and G. C. Steinhardt. 1984. *Indiana soils and landscapes.* Publication AV-250. Cooperative Extension Service, Purdue University, West Lafayette, Indiana.
9. Gillette, D. A. 1986. *Wind erosion.* In *Soil Conservation: Assessing the National Resources Inventory, Volume 2.* National Academy Press, Washington, D.C. pp. 129-158.
10. Larson, W. E., F. J. Pierce, and R. H. Dowdy. 1983. *The threat of soil erosion to long-term crop production.* Science 219: 458-465.
11. Lovejoy, S. B., and T. L. Napier, editors. 1986. *Conserving soil: Insights from socioeconomic research.* Soil Conservation Society of America, Ankeny, Iowa. 155 pp.
12. Onstad, C. E., F. J. Pierce, R. H. Dowdy, and W. E. Larson. 1986. *Erosion and productivity interrelations on a soil landscape.* Transactions, American Society of Agricultural Engineers. 28(6): 1,885-1,888.
13. Pierce, F. J. 1986. *Modeling soil productivity changes due to erosion.* In *Proceedings, 13th International Soil Science Congress.* Wageningen, The Netherlands.
14. Pierce, F. J., R. H. Dowdy, W. E. Larson, and W. A. P. Graham. 1984. *Soil productivity in the Corn Belt: An assessment of erosion's long-term effects.* Journal of Soil and Water Conservation. 39(2): 131-136.
15. Pierce, F. J., W. E. Larson, and R. H. Dowdy. 1986. *Field estimates of C factors: How good are they and how do they affect calculations of erosion.* In *Soil Conservation: Assessing the National Resources Inventory, Volume 2.* National Academy Press, Washington, D. C.
16. Pierce, F. J., W. E. Larson, R. H. Dowdy, and W. A. P. Graham. 1983. *Production of soils: Assessing long-term changes due to erosion.* J. Soil and Water Conservation. 38(1): 39-44.

17. Runge, C. F., W. E. Larson, and G. Roloff. 1986. *Using productivity measures to target conservation programs: A comparative analysis.* Journal of Soil and Water Conservation 41(1): 45-49.

18. Sopher, C. D., and J. V. Baird. 1983. *Soils and soils management.* 2nd Edition. Reston Publishing Co., Inc. Reston, Va. 22090. 312 p.

19. Taff, S., and C. F. Runge. 1986. *Supply control, conservation and budget restraint: Conflicting instruments in the 1985 Farm Bill.* Staff paper P86-33. Department of Agriculture and Applied Economics, University of Minnesota, St. Paul.

3

Information management[1]

Chris J. Johannsen

Since World War II, the United States has been in the throes of change that many refer to as the "information revolution." Author Alvin Toffler (6), in his book *The Third Wave,* described three waves or revolutions that have radically changed the course of history, human condition, and destinies of nations. The first wave, according to Toffler, is that long sweep of history from the time a woman (the first farmer) first planted a seed in the soil and agriculture was born, perhaps 15,000 years ago, until the beginning of the industrial revolution, the second wave 300 years ago.

Toffler suggested that the third wave of dramatic change in human history is now under way. This wave, he said, is characterized by revolutionary changes in communication and information flow. It is also a time, he said, when we must reexamine our use of resources and our relationships to our environment, our lifestyles, and our ineffective political processes of crisis management as we confront one dilemma after another.

An important aspect that obscures our understanding of the use of our resources, especially land, is that societies around the world that occupy and use land still operate across the broad spectrum described by Toffler. Some still operate in the first wave, others in the second; only a few societies are beginning to use technologies and concepts of the third wave for developing, managing, and conserving natural resources. In the United States, for example, many federal and state agencies now make extensive use of the new technologies of remote sensing and geographic informa-

[1]Purduce University Agricultural Experiment Station Journal Paper No. 10991.

tion systems, which show great promise for inventorying and monitoring natural resources as well as providing decision-makers with useful data.

Geographic information systems

Geographic information systems are data management systems designed to collect, organize, and present specific information about cultural and natural resources. Many times the information is in the form of a map that identifies such features as soil types, property units, townships, watersheds, and transportation networks. Remotely sensed data, such as those obtained from aircraft and satellite systems, come from a variety of sensors resulting in a wide range of formats, levels of resolution, and quality.

Many resource managers have found that GIS provide a cost-effective approach for the planning, development, management, and conservation of natural resources. The systems have been rather expensive in the past, but new developments in hardware and software have brought about great cost reductions. A user, of course, must be aware of the quality of the data in the system and that database maintenance is essential for accurate, up-to-date information. More and more also, the user needs to be aware of data security. Some agencies are reluctant to share their information with other organizations or agencies because the data may be incriminating to specific landowners, there may be some inaccuracies known only to the data collector, or modifications may have been made in the data because of differences in data collections, either in time or spatial aspects.

Natural resource agencies in 32 states, beginning with New York in 1966, have seriously explored or initiated comprehensive approaches to resolving their data needs. While objectives vary, most states develop geographic databases or geographic information systems to serve specific purposes. GIS development is usually a painful process because of the need for agreement and coordination among state and federal agencies. Agencies oftentimes are reluctant to give up their data. Some are afraid also, if they are not in control of the system, that the data will not be useful for their purpose.

I was involved in Missouri's approach through the coordination of natural resource information that began in 1972 when a Governor's Committee on Remote Sensing was formed by the state agencies that used remote sensing products. The governor charged the committee with the responsibility of reviewing the remote sensing efforts in the state and asked for a plan to coordinate remote sensing activities in the future. After three months of biweekly meetings, the participants concluded that they not only lacked information about each other's remote sensing activities but also could share some technical data and information.

The name of the committee was changed to the Governor's Committee on Technical Data Sharing and discussions continued. Reorganization of state government in 1978 caused the name to be changed to the Interagency Council on Natural Resources Data Sharing. This name was later changed to Interdepartmental Council on Natural Resource Information, which finally became so deeply involved in discussions of objectives, membership, voting rights, and related subjects that the original purpose seemed in doubt and the group was disbanded.

A year or two later, an interagency group was organized to assist in the development of the Geographic Resources Center at the University of Missouri in Columbia. This group, now called the Geographic Resources Center Advisory Committee, provides guidance to the center on specific information needs as well as techniques for retrieving that information. The center's mission was established to (a) coordinate interagency applied research in remote sensing and spatial analysis, (b) provide expertise with development of statewide databases, and (c) establish a resource center for remote sensing in cartographic data sources and applications.

Information projects and programs

The best way to illustrate GIS use is to discuss projects that employ this approach. Remote sensing was used in a number of these projects. In many cases, however, it was only one of the sources of input to the GIS.

Land cover maps. Many users are able to separate land cover categories using Landsat satellite data from which they can interpret land use. Barney and associates (1) were able to separate grain crops, hay and pasture, as well as timber and urban categories using Landsat images at a scale of 1:250,000. These researchers used tonal differences and land patterns to help in the separation process, then verified their interpretations with aerial photography and ground observations.

Utility of these maps could be assessed from the helpful information their locational aspects conveyed. To the fertilizer or chemical company looking for dealer and distribution locations, the grain crop map showed where crops were located. The proportion of area in grain crops calculated from the maps reaffirmed U. S. Department of Agriculture figures. Agricultural workers, such as extension specialists, can use the locational information in program planning for more effective educational efforts. For example, a livestock specialist would know the location of cow-calf operations by observing hay and pasture distribution. A wildlife specialist could predict the location of specific animals or fowl based upon the relationship of timber to other cover categories.

The grain crop map looked similar to the prime agricultural land map for the same area. This was not surprising; farmers grow their most valuable cash crops on their best soils.

A citizens' group in Boone County was concerned about the loss of prime agricultural land due to coal mining activities, especially a proposed coal gasification plant that would have increased coal mining in the county. There were estimates ranging from several hundred acres to more than 20,000 acres of prime agricultural land being destroyed by the mining activity. We overlaid the prime agricultural land map with a map showing the mineable coal in the county and determined that 1,620 acres of prime agricultural land would be affected by the mining activity. Interestingly, when the committee became aware of that number and an explanation of how it was obtained, discussion then centered on the cost of reclaiming that amount of prime agricultural land rather than guessing further about how many acres would be affected. Planning groups, agency personnel, and private individuals will tend to use accurate, timely, and reliable information in a proper manner if they are given the information, along with a brief explanation of how it was obtained.

Wildlife habitat evaluation. Projects have been completed in conjunction with the Missouri Department of Conservation and the Soil Conservation Service to examine pheasant, deer, and turkey habitats in a number of areas within the state. One project used Landsat data to look at pheasant habitat in a county in northwestern Missouri. A June 5, 1980, Landsat frame was used to provide maps and data on row crop, hay and pasture, forest, and wetland areas. It was soon noted that the acreage of row crops (corn, soybeans, and sorghum) increased greatly during a five-year time span. The row crop acreage in 1980 comprised more than 70 percent of the county, while five years previously USDA figures showed this acreage to be 47 percent of the county.

Data collected by wildlife biologists on the locations of pheasants were placed in the dataset, as were data obtained from rural mail carriers who cooperated by marking the locations where they saw or heard pheasants while on their routes. This information was then related to the ratio of row crop acreage to hay and pasture areas. Biologists never before had this type of detailed information available to them, and it has led them to question some of the previously accepted ratios they thought were the most ideal for pheasant habitat.

This study also found that timber habitat had declined more than 7 percent, to less than 3 percent of the county, during the same five years. The loss of timber correlated closely with the significant decline in deer killed during hunting seasons over the same period.

When the center's advisory committee viewed the information compiled about this county, SCS personnel noted a significant increase in soil erosion in the same county. The loss of pasture acres and the dramatic increase in row crops on rolling land provided specific information needed by SCS technicians. Not only were they able to locate areas of severe erosion, they were also able to adjust their manpower needs to assist in the soil conservation effort.

When an agribusiness representative viewed the data, it was noted that there was a significant shortage of elevator space and railroad cars to move grain crops from the area during the previous several years. Moreover, the potential for fertilizer and chemical sales had increased dramatically. Such specific data for all counties would have been advantageous to any industry dealing with the sale of agricultural supplies and products.

An agricultural meteorologist viewing the data questioned if the changing cropping patterns in the area could have a significant impact on climatic patterns in the region. Changes in evapotranspiration and loss of moisture at different times of the year could affect rainfall intensities and timing.

The most interesting point of having different advisory committee members view the same data was that each of them interpreted the same data based upon their own backgrounds and experiences. The maps showing the locational aspects of the data contributed significantly to their understanding and interpretations.

Watershed inventory. Several projects were completed that required development of the GIS to obtain specific information over a watershed or drainage area. One of the first of these projects, in Chariton County, Missouri, was initiated by SCS working with the Laboratory for Applications of Remote Sensing at Purdue University (7). This project used Landsat data to map land cover and overlaid this information with digitized township, watershed, and physiographic position maps.

The physiographic maps enabled the display of Landsat land cover categories by landscape positions, including bottomlands, gently sloping uplands, and moderately steep uplands. Use of this information illustrated that one could make maps showing land cover by specific subwatershed areas and supply the acreage of each cover type within a watershed. Further work with SCS showed that the data were useful for estimating runoff and sediment yields from a watershed during a certain time period or from a specific rainstorm.

Other projects involving SCS and the Geographic Resources Center led to detailed analysis of specific watersheds, including development of slope categories from U.S. Geological Survey 7½-minute topographic maps. The slope categories were 0 to 5 percent, 5 to 9 percent, 9 to 14 percent, greater than 14 percent, and bottomland. Subwatersheds also have been digitized within a major watershed so that specific data could be obtained, such as land cover type for an entire watershed, land cover maps by slope categories, and subwatershed maps showing land cover information. Soils data have been digitized as well and placed into the database whenever it was available for analysis of the watershed. Efforts on watershed analysis have continued because project engineers and planners have specific data needs that often lead to the development of new techniques for retrieving the needed information.

National resource inventory. In 1981 SCS held a meeting with state and federal resource agencies, farm organizations, and the University of Missouri to assess these groups' resource information needs. As a result, Missouri expanded the data collection format of the proposed National Resources Inventory to include more detailed wildlife habitat and timber resource data. In addition, at the request of the participants, the data were put into a geographically referenced database to respond to queries in graphic, map, and tabular formats (*3*). The Geographic Resources Center developed the NRI geographic database under contract with USDA.

The sample selected for the 1982 NRI in Missouri included more than 13,000 primary sample units (PSUs). These represented a sample of about 4 percent and translated to 150 PSUs for an average Missouri county. Because three sample locations were selected statistically within each PSU, data were collected at 39,000 locations by SCS soil scientists and district conservationists, providing the most detailed data ever collected on Missouri's soil and water resources (*2*).

Details of the data entry and verification, digitizing of PSU locations, digitizing of ancillary data, and implementation of a retrieval and display system are provided elsewhere (*4*). Seven statewide maps were digitized for inclusion in the database; they serve as supplemented geocodes for improving the analytical and reporting functions of the NRI geographic information system. Digitized maps included general soils, county boundaries, forest cover, zoology regions, fish-fauna regions, major land resource areas, and hydrologic units. A database management system integrates the PSU field data, PSU locations, supplemental attribute geocodes, and supplementary attribute boundary files.

SCS and the Missouri Department of Natural Resources are currently requesting specific illustration and results from the Missouri PSU database. In August 1984 Missouri voters approved a sales tax of one-tenth of one percent to provide state funds for a cost-sharing program as an incentive to landowners to use more conservation practices. Funds are administrated through the Department of Natural Resources, with SCS providing technical assistance. Funds are to be used when USDA Agricultural Stabilization and Conservation Service funds are not available for erosion control practices. Therefore, soil and water conservation districts are cooperating with ASCS county committees in the program.

Census data base development. Geographic information systems can also contain social and economic data so long as they have geographic attributes. The Missouri State Senate asked the Geographic Resources Center to digitize the 1980 census maps of Missouri and merge this information with census population data tapes provided by the U.S. Census Bureau. The motivation for this effort was to give the Senate staff the ability to draw proposed reapportionment maps interactively on the computer screen and provide population statistics for each district drawn.

The computer was not to redistrict the state or draw redistricting lines. Instead it was to provide a fast and accurate method for determining the population characteristics within given district boundaries. A number of redistricting plans were run at various times for the Senate committee, including a live demonstration for several state senators during a visit to the center.

In the end the overall problem of redrawing the district boundaries to eliminate some districts could not be solved by the Senate. The redistricting boundaries had to be established by the courts in late 1981. The courts did, however, use the results of a number of maps that had been analyzed by this procedure.

The census information has been used by other groups within the state. Missouri's Extension Service used the maps to determine total population and population characteristics in each of the 20 extension districts within the state. SCS used the information in a similar manner to arrive at numbers for the nine SCS areas. It has been suggested that Census of Agriculture data could be put in the same format and provide useful planning information for many agricultural agencies.

Missouri fish and wildlife information system. A database management system describing fish and wildlife species in Missouri was completed with information on more than 725 species. All information for these species was entered into species booklets, then coded, key-entered, verified, translated into readily readable booklets, and loaded into a database management system known as Stanford Public Information Retrieval Systems (SPIRES).

Biologists from the different agencies can access the database remotely from their office locations. The system can provide responses to queries, such as which fowl species are likely to be found in the nesting stage during the first two weeks of April in Greene County. This information would be useful if somebody were planning to do construction work in the area and wanted to avoid causing problems for particular species, especially those on the endangered species list.

A look to the future

The potential usefulness of geographic information systems seems limited only by funding and the imagination of those working with the system. Existing systems have been used for a variety of projects, such as an inventory or assessment of forest cover, agricultural crops, and wildlife habitat; the monitoring of forest conversions and timber harvesting, water resources or urban development; and the analysis of land impacts and mined land reclamation.

The future promises development of better methods of collecting data, such as the 10-meter-resolution data collected by the French satellite, SPOT. Further research and development will bring about more timely, cost-effective techniques and procedures. There will be more flexibility in data selection, more versatility in data analysis procedures, and better distribution systems with a variety of graphic and map products. One can tailor maps, tables, and graphs to the user's need. Officials must be aware of the training opportunities for bringing more users into contact with these analytic procedures. Data from many different time periods can be compared, establishing trends and changes useful for the prediction of changes in natural resources.

Technology can help manage data and information about cultural and natural resources. We need only plan the use of limited resources, starting with meeting the information needs of professional workers and decision-makers.

REFERENCES

1. Barney, T.W., C.J. Johannsen, and D.J. Barr. 1977. *Mapping land use from satellite images - a users guide.* Marshall Space Flight Center, National Aeronautics and Space Administration, Huntsville, Alabama. 44 pp.
2. Johannsen, C.J., 1984. *Missouri's National Resources Inventory.* University of Missouri, Columbia, Agronomy Technical Report 2(11): 2-7.
3. Johannsen, C.J. 1986. *Potential uses of the NRI in state and local decision making.* In *Soil Conservation: Assessing the National Resources Inventory, Volume 2.* National Academy Press, Washington, D.C. pp. 296-308.
4. Johannsen, C.J., J.M. Pan, T.W. Barney, and G.T. Koeln. 1984. *A database information system for Missouri's National Resource Inventory.* In Proceedings, Pecora IX Symposium. Earth Resources Observation System, Sioux Falls, South Dakota. pp. 25-28.
5. Mead, D.A. 1981. *Statewide natural resource information systems.* Journal of Forestry 79:369-372.
6. Toffler, Alvin. 1980. *The third wave.* William Morrow & Co., New York, New York. 537 pp.
7. Weismiller, R.A., I.D. Persinger, and O.L. Montgomery. 1977. *Soil survey from digital analysis of satellite sensor and topographic data.* Soil Science Society America Journal 42:1166-1170.

4

Implementation of soil and water conservation policy

Peter J. Nowak

The conservation provisions of the Food Security Act of 1985 have been hailed as the beginning of a new era for conservation. These provisions attempt to link land protection with commodity support programs. Conservation compliance, a provision making agricultural financial incentives contingent upon appropriate conservation behavior, represents the introduction of a new dimension to conservation policy. The traditional voluntary approach has now been bolstered by a form of cross-compliance. Policy analysts, conservationists, and environmentalists all are optimistic about this new direction for conservation policy.

Federal, state, and local conservation administrators also have an opportunity to select more accurate targeting criteria for soil and water conservation programs. The National Resources Inventory, coupled with erosion productivity loss models (25, 26), indices of erosion vulnerability (9, 17, 22), and models that estimate erosion-induced nonpoint-source pollution (3, 4) can form the basis for more effective conservation policy. Research underlying these models has established that objective criteria can be used to determine which land areas should be taken from production or otherwise protected. Although certain technical issues remain to be resolved (11), there is widespread consensus that targeting for conservation program resources on the basis of these technical criteria is feasible.

Yet the ability to design and target conservation policy using either commodity program participation or technical criteria will not, by themselves, produce an effective conservation policy. In essence, generating objective information for targeting is one process; designing a policy around this data is another; while managing an organizational system to implement the resulting programs is still another. No conservation policy, no matter how promising or scientifically valid, will protect even one acre until it is implemented.

Until now conservation policy has been driven by what may be called the "better mousetrap" principle of conservation. This principle contends that if a conservation problem can be adequately documented, if practices exist that are physically capable of addressing this problem, and if financial assistance is available for using these practices, then they will be used. In other words, the emphasis has been on the design and specification of the mousetrap with little attention being given to whether it can actually catch a mouse. Although sounding ludicrous when presented in this fashion, the fact remains that the process of implementation is underemphasized, misunderstood, and generally ignored in the analysis of conservation policies. Past emphasis has been on better specification of the problem or design of innovation conservation policy. It has been assumed that implementation will "catch" the appropriate landusers if these antecedents can be specified.

The implementation process

A review of the soil and water conservation literature demonstrates that little is known, or at least reported, about the implementation of conservation policy. Political scientists have long recognized that implementation is crucial to the success of any policy or program (19). In contrast to this basic tenet of political science, we have thousands of studies on specifying natural resource problems, more on the design of alternative conservation policies, but very few on the implementation process within the soil and water conservation establishment. This disregard has obscured the critical role that implementation plays in determining conservation policy effectiveness.

What determines the effectiveness of conservation policy? Explanations of variation in the effectiveness of conservation policy coalesce around three general themes. The most popular explanation is that the design of a policy influences its effectiveness. Policy analysts argue that we need to redesign or modify policies to shift the mix of regulations, cross-compliance provisions, and financial or technical assistance in order to make the resulting programs more effective. The logic behind this explanation is that the program must be made more congruent to the market forces currently influencing landuser decisions.

A second school of thought argues that specificity in defining the nature of a problem will influence policy effectiveness. Increased understanding of the incidence and cause of resource degradation allow administrators to focus limited conservation dollars on the high priority situations. The design of the policy does not need to change under this scenario. Instead, it is argued that the effectiveness of any resulting program will increase if it can be applied in a more precise manner.

Third, and the argument advanced in this chapter, is that irregularities in implementation processes will influence policy effectiveness. Variation in effectiveness occurs when the resulting program is implemented differently across similar settings. This happens when political processes and administrative mediocrity distort the translation of a policy into programs that are accessible and understandable to landusers. Implementation, then, focuses on the ''front line'' of the conservation arena, where the political decisions and academic interpretations need to be translated into recommendations for specific landusers. Or as one environmental administrator put it, ''There is an old adage here. You can declare war in Washington, but you have got to run it in the field'' (*12*).

The first school of thought focuses on the nature of conservation policy and resulting programs, the second on where the resulting programs are used, and the third on how the policy is translated into a program and implemented. Rather than treating these as competing, all three explanations need to be integrated in a holistic fashion. A proposed relationship among these three explanations of conservation policy effectiveness is presented in figure 1. This diagram attempts to portray the cyclical relationship between policy design, resulting conservation programs, the natural resource base, and information management processes. Beginning at the bottom of figure 1, characteristics of soil and water resources, including genesis and degradation processes, are investigated through basic science research. Determining the prevalence of these processes in the larger environment is the role of various assessment and inventory procedures. These assessments are then coupled with models to develop future scenarios on the status of the natural resource base. Information management continues as these model outputs are used as input to political and administrative processes associated with designing conservation policy. The policy is then translated into adminstrative rules, and agency responsibilities are specified. The outcome of this process can be considered a conservation program as opposed to the more general policy. These conservation programs are then transmitted down through organizational hierarchies to local agency representatives in the form of implementation guidelines or

strategies. A critical feature is the capability of these local agency representatives to communicate and administer the program with the desired target
audience. The rate of program acceptance influences landuser activities,
which, in turn, begins the cycle anew by affecting the natural resource base.

This diagram exemplifies implementation as a critical element in the
conservation policy process. Information generated on erosion vulnerability
or erosion-induced nonpoint-source pollution needs to be designed with
implementation in mind. Quite clearly more information or innovative
policy options, by themselves, are worthless unless we have the capacity
to translate and transmit it to those parties whose actions it is intended
to influence.

At issue is understanding the translation and transmission of information and policy options to the appropriate landusers. The extent to which
this is occuring is a research issue, not an assumption guiding policy
analysis. This requires one to recognize that translating a policy into programs and then implementing those programs are both largely determined
by political situations among the responsible conservation organizations.
After all, program implementation has been defined as the continuation

Figure 1. The conservation policy process.

of the politics that originally formulated the policy (*1*). Political and organizational processes need to be recognized as influencing both the design and implementation of conservation policy.

Dimensions of the implementation process. Policies are implemented by organizations. Organizations charged with implementing a policy often assume defensive positions. A significant amount of effort goes into "maneuvering to avoid responsibility, scrutiny, and blame" (*1*). In addition, many of these same organizations have developed long-term constituencies among landusers. Different implementation strategies are often evaluated on the responses by these vested constituents rather than on the effect on the resource problem in question. These general observations from political science imply that there are two key dimensions of the implementation process relative to conservation organizations: their relations with each other and their relationships with landusers.

Interorganizational relations. Implementation is concerned with how an idea is translated into effective collective action. Due to the fragmentation of responsibilities among U.S. Department of Agriculture agencies and the existence of autonomous and semi-autonomous organizations across different levels of government, interorganizational relations are more important than intraorganizational transactions. Explaining variation in the effectiveness of conservation policy due to implementation is predicated upon understanding how all the relevant conservation organizations work together.

The current status of interorganizational relations is dominated by the assumption that the responsible organizations are working together to implement conservation policy. Federal agencies are assumed to be coordinating their actions with state and local counterparts. The validity of this assumption is highly suspect. It needs to be questioned because the traditional inclination has been to ignore or avoid the organizational issues associated with addressing natural resource problems. At best they are recognized as "agency squabbles" or "political tinkering" with the conservation system. At worst these organizational issues are treated as trivial or reduced to fatuous statements about the coordination among various agency "black boxes" found on federal and state organizational charts. Hopefully, it does not come as too much of a shock to note that the conflict, competition, and censorious behavior that has characterized conservation organizations through the last 50 years continues unabated today (*23*).

There has been little research within the conservation arena on these interorganizational issues (7, 10, 13, 18, 21). What has occurred has found that coordination largely occurs on a haphazard basis. It has been observed that coordination at the local level is almost entirely dependent upon the informal, interpersonal relations that may or may not emerge among organizational principals. Coordination, it appears, has neither priority nor support among organizational administrators. While receiving an ample amount of platitudinous support and other forms of "lip service," the fact remains that the majority of agency personnel at the local operational level find themselves in the self-taught, sink-or-swim school of coordination. Interorganizational coordination is neither easy to achieve nor free of costs. It requires a significant, initial investment of organizational resources in order to gain long-term efficiencies. Since there has been little political support for this initial investment, coordination continues to be an assumption guiding whatever conservation programs may be in place.

In terms of implementation, coordination can occur from the top down, or from the bottom up. Historically, this has happened from the top down due to the time of development of the conservation organizations. Agencies such as the Soil Conservation Service and the Agricultural Stabilization and Conservation Service have been able to determine most conservation activities at the local level through their traditional line-control of conservation funding and personnel. However, soil conservation districts theoretically should be serving as the coordinator for all local conservation activities. In other words, serving as a countervailing power for bottom-up coordination. This is due to the broad range of powers and authority vested in them through the state statutes that responded to the 1937 Standard State and Soil Conservation District Law. The district also receives support from state and federal conservation agencies that rely on the district for local legitimacy. All this implies that the district has a tremendous potential to coalesce and coordinate conservation activities by state and federal organizations.

Unfortunately, this has largely failed to happen. Many farmers, the target of any coordinated implementation effort, fail to recognize that their conservation district even exists (2). When they do recognize the local district, it is often viewed as little more than a farmer advisory board to SCS. Most importantly, even the agencies whose activities the districts should be coordinating are confused about or reluctant to acknowledge the identity and functions of conservation districts (7).

The National Association of Conservation Districts has been an effective ally of SCS in promoting support for conservation programs and in particular for SCS. NACD has, however, been much less successful in channeling national resources to and within its own organization, that is, state associations and local districts. While recognized as an effective advocate for the conservation cause at the national level, NACD has remained relatively inert in lobbying for issues affecting state associations or local districts. Further, the trend toward increased local and state responsibility for conservation programs has put NACD in the difficult position of supporting SCS at the national level while also promoting the independence of the local district employees who are often in direct competition with SCS district conservationists.

This brief description of relations among conservation organizations is an attempt to establish the critical role these relations play in determining the effectiveness of any conservation policy. Implementation of conservation policy can be translated into the maneuvering of these semi-autonomous actors located at different levels of government, where each is seeking to protect its domain while also expanding its control into areas controlled by others. These interorganizational relations, in turn, influence their relations to landusers.

Organizations and landusers. The second key dimension of implementation is the interface between organizations with conservation responsibilities and the landuser. These agencies must perform three general functions in working with landusers as part of the process of implementing policy. First, they must formulate strategies to get landowners to recognize the symptoms and causes of the resource degradation specified within the policy. Second, as these causes are identified, they have to educate the landuser about alternative land uses recommended and supported under current conservation programs and plans. Third, they must assist landusers in designing and installing the conservation systems supported by the policy. As will be seen, conservation organizations have focused mainly on the third of these three functions.

Imagine any agricultural industry trying to sell a product without explaining and demonstrating to the producer why it is needed. Sales would be dismal. Why should things be any different for conservation? Agency effectiveness at getting landusers to recognize resource problems, or the need for participation in conservation programs, is very poor. Part of the inefficiency in this first function is due to the actions of the conservation establishment, and part is due to increasing sophistication in specifying what constitutes a resource problem. Relative to this latter situation, it was fairly easy to develop problem recognition when one could point to significant productivity losses on a field prior to the introduction of commercial fertilizer or to the horizon darkened by blowing soil, as in the 1930s. Yet specifying when and how erosion is considered a problem is much more complex today (5, 24).

There are other reasons for the failure of landusers to recognize the need for conservation programs. The research literature has pointed out that a significant number of farmers misperceive their erosion problems (2, 8, 14). This misperception is partially due to the continued preoccupation of the conservation establishment with the "Big Gully Crusade" over the last 50 years. It is dramatic and easy to communicate resource degradation when focusing on the most severe cases. It is also largely inaccurate. This emphasis on the big gullies while ignoring the more prevalent sheet, rill, and ephemeral gully erosion has been counterproductive in convincing landusers that they may have erosion problems. In the farmer's mind no gully implies no problem and no problem implies no need to check out the details on conservation programs.

A second reason for failing to get more landusers to recognize a need for conservation programs is the artificial distinction that has been created and maintained between production agriculture and resource conservation. Private and public organizations have traditionally treated conservation as something that may be added on to a production system rather than managed as an integral part of it. USDA agencies (especially the Cooperative Extension Service), land grant universities, and the private agricultural sector have a deficient record when it comes to promoting a sustainable agriculture. While advocating a philosophy of maximizing production to address market dilemmas, they have largely ignored the short- and long-term consequences for both the natural resource base and the producer. Thus, landusers who are caught up in this production treadmill rarely have the opportunity to develop an interest in soil and water conservation as an integral part of agriculture.

A third reason for a low rate of problem recognition is the passive approach traditionally taken by conservation organizations. Although there has been noted improvement in recent years, usually these organizations work with those requesting assistance rather than seeking out those landusers who most need assistance. The recent transition to policies focused on critical areas should further assist in the elimination of the first-come, first-served approach to local conservation assistance.

The current status of the second element of the organization-landuser interface is not much better. Conservation organizations, as part of the implementation process, must educate landusers about conservation practices and how to work with the system in order to receive support in adopting recommended practices. Yet one study (*16*) found that farmers were very poorly informed about institutional support for these practices. This study found only two-thirds (69.3%) of the farmers believing that the government would cost-share terraces even when local monies were available. Terraces were practices that were both applicable and needed in the study area. Furthermore, as seen in table 1, only 20 percent of the farmers correctly knew the cost-sharing rate for these terraces. Twice as many farmers (42%) did not know the cost-share rate, and there was significant variation in estimates, from 5 to 90 percent cost-sharing rates, among the remaining farmers. Although it is difficult to generalize from such a small sample, it is one indication that landusers are poorly informed about the support they will receive under conservation programs.

But informing landusers about these programs is difficult because of the wide variation among landusers in managerial ability, size of the agricultural operation controlled, economic viability, awareness and knowledge of degradation processes, level of participation in other

Table 1. Farmers estimates of government cost-sharing available for terraces.

Percent Cost-Share	Number	Percent
5 - 30	5	3
31 - 50	17	12
51 - 74	8	6
75*	28	20
76 - 90	23	17
Don't Know	59	42
Totals	140	100

* Accurate cost-share rate

Table 2. Farmer estimated cost of 100 feet of terrace on own field.

Total Dollar Estimate	Number	Percent
25 - 99	4	3
100 - 250	7	5
251 - 450	6	4
451 - 600	11	8
601 - 750	3	2
751 - 1250	10	7
1251 - 1500	1	1
1501 - 2500	8	6
2501 - 5000	6	4
5001 - 10,000	3	2
Don't know	80	58
Totals	139	100

Table 3. Farmer estimated costs of conservation practices. *

Conservation Practice	Percent Able To Provide Estimate	Mean Estimate	Range of Estimates†
Crop rotation	18.5	$41.09	$1 - 600
Conservation tillage	17.1	$40.32	$1 - 5,000
No-tillage	18.8	$405.70	$1 - 10,000
Contour stripcropping	16.8	$19.22	$2 - 100
Contour farming	16.4	$61.72	$2 - 2,000
Winter cover crop	18.8	$26.12	$1 - 400
Terrace system	13.7	$371.80	$4 - 9,000
Shelterbelts	14.7	$70.39	$3 - 1,000
Waterway	18.5	$114.80	$1 - 2,000

*N of sample = 292
†Range of estimates does not include those respondents who gave "zero" as a response because they had already adopted the practice or believed there would be no costs.

assistance programs, planning horizon, and the organization of the production unit, among others. Conservation organizations need to be able to work with this variation rather than falling into the pattern of treating all landusers as an uniform, homogenous, mass of rational economic actors. Landusers are neither a uniform group nor do they evaluate conservation practices solely on the basis of economic rationality.

This lack of economic rationality is partly due to the failure of the conservation agencies to inform landusers about the basic economics of conservation practices. Some evidence of this lack of economic information comes from the same study mentioned earlier (*16*). Farmers were asked to provide their best estimate of the cost of 100 feet of terrace on their land. A summary of their responses is found in table 2. Some of the variation in table 2 is to be expected because of differences in soil, topography, and the type of terrace the farmers used in their estimate. However, the fact remains that more than half the farmers (58 percent) had no idea of costs, even after they were asked for an estimate with three different techniques. Even more important is the finding that only 5 percent of the farmers fell within the range of $1.00 to $2.50 per lineal foot given as an average estimate by local technicians.

Further evidence of this lack of basic economic information comes from a larger study in Wisconsin (*6*). Farmers in this study were asked to assume they had to install a list of practices in order to be eligible for a conservation program. They were then asked to give a per acre estimate of the installation costs of these conservation practices. The results are presented in table 3. The distribution in table 3 provides additional evidence that a majority of farmers are ignorant of the costs of common conservation practices. And of those who do have estimates, there is a tendency to significantly overestimate the perceived costs of conservation practices. This might be due to the near-Pavlovian response we have developed among farmers during the last 50 years. If we mention conservation practices, then they expect financial cost-sharing regardless of the inherent profitability of or need for the practice. There is another potential explanation for the ignorance exemplified in tables 2 and 3. Informing and educating the farmer about the economics of conservation has traditionally received a very low priority among agencies with responsibilities for implementing conservation policy and, in particular, the Cooperative Extension Service. Not only have the agencies failed to inform farmers about basic economic facts, the agencies have even failed to generate the interest necessary to seek out these facts, assuming they were available. Thus, the findings in tables 2 and 3 are probably more the result of agency actions or inactions than they are a reflection of the capability of the landusers.

The third element of the organization-landuser interface is the provision of assistance in installing and maintaining the conservation practices. A very different picture emerges here. Research evidence (2) shows that those farmers who are finally brought into the system and have overcome the obstacles to understanding the need and cost of conservation practices are very satisfied with the assistance they receive. Here, the organization-landuser interface in the implementation of conservation policy is functioning at its best.

This second dimension of the implementation process, the conservation organization-landuser interface, has also lacked attention in the analysis of conservation policy. A reason for this is the assumption of uniformity in the implementation of any conservation policy. Somehow we have come to believe that a policy written in Washington, D.C. or some state capital implies the uniform and comprehensive receipt of the resulting program provisions by landusers. Policies are then evaluated by comparing their features relative to the acceptance rate by landusers. Poor performance is attributed to inappropriate policy features. Yet somewhere in this rational analysis we have forgotten or purposely ignored the less-than-perfect market faced by the landuser. As long as conservation organizations continue to ignore their responsibility to inform landusers of such basic facts as the need for and estimated cost of conservation practices, conservation policy will continue to be ineffective. The often-reported "failure" of the voluntary approach may have more to do with the incompetence of the organizations with conservation responsibilities than with the landusers who are responding to this much-less-than-perfect information market.

It is difficult to imagine any conservation policy being effective when the majority of landusers fail to recognize a need for remedial actions, are ignorant of the basic economic facts surrounding the recommended practices, and are confused about the identities and functions of the responsible conservation agencies.

Implementation strategies

The preceding discussion attempted to establish that implementation is an important part of the policy cycle portrayed in figure 1. Efficient use of scientific and technological information in protecting the natural resource base is dependent upon understanding the institutional arrangements responsible for generating, interpreting, and disseminating this knowledge. Central to this process is the need to recognize that conservation interorganizational relations and organization-landuser interfaces can also be viewed as a *cause* of continued natural resource problems. Further infusions of technological innovations or capital do not address the underlying inefficiencies in current institutional arrangements. These inefficiencies are most apparent when examining implementation processes. Attention to implementation processes shifts the focus from the landuser, or the soil and water resource base, to the organizations responsible for working with these elements.

Three different strategies exist to improve the implementation process: first, put more emphasis on building the capacity of conservation districts to develop the leadership necessary to coordinate local conservation implementation activities; second, provide flexible policy tools to respond to the diversity found among landusers; and third, develop criteria and procedures to evaluate the organizations responsible for implementing conservation policies.

Building the capacity of conservation districts. The capability of soil conservation districts to direct local conservation activities can be a major influence on the ultimate effectiveness in implementing any conservation policy. As noted earlier, conservation districts, until now, have been largely co-opted by SCS. Right or wrong, the fact of the matter is that SCS has been able to implicitly or explicitly direct local district activities. During the early years of conservation districts, this arrangement was beneficial in nurturing and developing district capabilities. It is questionable, however, whether this relationship is still in the best interests of resource conservation.

The difficulty with this arrangement is that it precludes one of the two models for coordinating the activities of organizations with conservation responsibilities. One model, the top-down approach, has all the federal organizations (SCS, ASCS, CES, Farmers Home Administration, etc.) working out coordination arrangements at the national level. These agreements are then independently transmitted down through the respective organizational hierarchies to the local level. Coordination between the local respresentatives of these organizations supposedly follows. Because the conservation district is not involved in these agreements, its current status, as described earlier, is the logical outcome. More importantly, because the coordinating mechanism is so distant (Washington, D.C.), local organizational actors often give these national agreements a low priority. The general coordination agreements reached at the national level rarely have enough flexibility to accommodate the diverse and unique situations found at the local level.

An alternative model is a bottom-up approach in which the conservation district assumes a leadership role. District representatives being locally elected officials have a significant amount of authority and persuasive power relative to the other conservation organizations. SCS is involved in the district only through the invitation of the district; districts are often formally linked or have shared representation with ASCS county committees; and the conservation district has the capability of providing a strong input to the locally-driven, county extension plans of work. The point is that the conservation district has the potential to provide the leadership in coordinating local conservation activities. Unfortunately, in large part this leadership has failed to materialize (15).

How can leadership in the conservation districts be developed to insure coordination of local conservation activities and, consequently, increase the effectiveness of implementing conservation policy? The social science literature is replete with examples of how to build the capacity of local governmental units. But it is difficult to apply this body of knowledge until the local governmental unit begins to recognize that it is indeed a subunit of the state, with special powers delegated by the state legislature to serve an important public purpose, not a "rubber stamp" that merely legitimizes the activities of other organizations. In short, the conservation district needs to recognize it is a governing body. Therefore, the recommendation advanced only addresses this critical first step: instilling the recognition that conservation districts have both the authority and the responsibility to coordinate the implementation of conservation programs.

Environmental and urban-based coalitions served as an effective countervailing power to vested commercial agricultural commodity interests in developing the conservation provisions of the 1985 farm bill. Discouragingly, these national countervailing powers have failed to use their state and local chapters to press for effective implementation of these same provisions at the district level. Being disciples of the "better mousetrap" principle of conservation, their main concern has been on the design of conservation policy at the national level. This does not have to be the case. These nonagricultural groups could begin working with state associations and local districts to help reassert the implementation and coordination expectations of the conservation districts. A generalization emerging from health, social services, and transportation policies has been the need for local pressure groups to monitor and evaluate the agencies responsible for implementation. Currently, there is no one monitoring the activities of conservation organizations at the local level. Due to the increasing awareness and documentation of the off-site damages of excessive soil erosion, there is a need for a local partnership between environmental and urban-based groups with the conservation districts.

A second need is for the major conservation organizations to acknowledge and act on the fact that the conservation district is there to direct and not just legitimize their presence. This does not mean that the local representatives of these organizations have to surrender their autonomy. SCS can still be responsible for technical standards, ASCS for establishing eligibility criteria for cost-sharing, and CES for agronomic and economic recommendations on conservation practices. However, these organizations need to acknowledge that the conservation district has the authority to establish priorities on where this assistance will be directed and in defining the responsibilities of each conservation organization relative to meeting those priorities. Of course, some will argue that this is already the case. Theoretically, that may be so but in actuality it is rare. Therefore, it should become the responsibility of each of these organizations, as well as NACD, to insure that this theoretical opportunity becomes a reality. Communications and training sessions need to be developed for conservation district representatives that specify their coordination role and responsibilities relative to other conservation organizations.

Third, NACD needs to begin using its lobbying power to garner national resources to build the capability of its constituents, conservation districts. This lobbying effort needs to be refocused from supporting other conservation organizations who work with the district to one where the priority is on the district. Conservation districts must have competent, assertive, well-educated, and trained staff members of their own selection and hiring to maintain their local program identity and continuity. Furthermore, NACD needs to become a more vocal spokesperson for the conservation districts at the national, regional, and state levels relative to relationships with the other conservation organizations. Conservation districts need a regional or national association that is a strong supporter of district authority and responsibility relative to the other conservation organizations. Any partnership, conservation or otherwise, needs more than a common objective. It also needs clear agreements between the partners on their relationships and responsibilities to each other.

Finally, there are a series of possible legal arrangements that would clarify and formalize the district's role. Agreements between state associations of districts could be made with state departments of agriculture, natural resources, or conservation. In turn, NACD could begin to develop similar legal agreements with USDA relative to the role of the conservation district. One final suggestion would be to amend state soil conservation laws that were based on the Standard State and Soil Conservation District Law in such a way that the leadership responsibilities of the districts are clarified.

Local policy flexibility. As we move to a system where the conservation organization-landuser interface is determined more by characteristics of the resource base, then the diversity of reasons for nonadoption of conservation practices will increase. This will happen because the current bias of working only with receptive landusers will be negated. Two responses are needed in this situation. First, understanding must be increased among local conservation personnel about the diversity of reasons that may account for the nonadoption decision. Second, once local personnel begin to understand this diversity, they will need program tools to address this situation effectively.

A diverse set of policy tools is needed to counter the traditional mentality that farmers can be voluntarily bribed into conservation behavior. Although our sophistication has increased recently to where we promise to withhold other payments for the lack of conservation behavior, this still does not match the diversity of reasons given by farmers for nonadoption. This diversity is simplified and portrayed in figure 2. Nonadopters of conservation practices fall into two general categories: those unwilling to adopt and those unable to adopt. Under each of these categories are two subcategories. This simple framework attempts to capture the complexity of reasons a landuser may have for nonadoption of conservation recommendations.

Those unwilling to adopt do so because of goal conflict or rational ignorance. Goal conflict refers to a situation where an operator views other goals, such as profit maximization or perceived sanctity of private property rights, as more important than conservation. Of course, this choice of one goal over another may be based on insufficient information. The data presented in tables 2 and 3 exemplify this situation. But in a "pure" case of goal conflict, the appropriate policy response would be regulation. Cross-compliance provisions with other incentives (e.g., USDA feed grain program) could be considered a weak form of regulation. Because these conservation compliance provisions are not universally applicable due to limited and variable participation in USDA programs, additional forms of regulation will be needed. However, as will be seen, regulation is appropriate only in cases of goal conflict.

Landusers can also be unwilling to adopt conservation practices because of a situation that may be characterized as rational ignorance (Tables 2 and 3). Rational ignorance is not a pejorative term in that it connotes a situation where one has not had the opportunity to learn. In this case it is often rational to remain ignorant because the costs of gathering the necessary information to make a certain decision exceed the apparent potential benefits of the decision. For example, assume the typical landuser attempted to answer the question, "Does conservation pay relative to my situation?" If this landuser has to work through a morass of agency referrals because of the local confusion over agency responsibilities and if the result of this run-around was only a series of vague, general answers, then the landuser is likely to conclude that there is neither the time nor the resources to pursue an adequate answer to this question. The policy response in this case is to design a conservation information transfer system that is more effec-

Causes For Nonadoption	Appropriate Program Strategies
Unwilling To Adopt Due To:	
Goal Conflict/Greed	Regulation
Rational Ignorance	Information Transfer
Unable To Adopt Due To:	
Complexity of System	Education
Recommendation Too Expensive	Cost-Sharing

Figure 2. Causes and strategies to nonadoption.

tive than the current one. The role of the conservation district in coordinating this system has been discussed previously.

In addition to being unwilling to adopt recommended conservation technologies, landusers may also be unable to adopt such technologies. Again, they may be unable to adopt for two reasons. The first concerns the complexity of integrating the conservation system into their overall production system. Adding conservation components (e.g., conservation tillage) to a production system that is already responding to climatic, pest, and policy cycles can become an insurmountable obstacle without appropriate educational assistance. Demonstrating that conservation can be an integral part of a production system is an educational function.

Until now we have relied on financial incentives to compensate for the risks, real or imagined, associated with integrating conservation into production systems. The proposed strategy is based on the premise that another method to reduce the perceived or real risk is education. Quite simply, it is a choice between paying someone to take a risk or to reduce the risk itself. It is in this area of reducing risk that local CES representatives would assume a major role. Educational activities on reducing the risk associated with using conservation practices is an appropriate response, at least in part, for those unable to adopt.

Landusers may also be unable to adopt because the recommended conservation practice is too expensive. This, of course, refers to the result of an objective cost-benefit analysis and not a conclusion reached through stereotype or ignorance as found in tables 2 and 3. The appropriate response in this case is to lower the conservation practice costs through a cost-sharing approach.

This schematic thus demonstrates that financial incentives, our traditional, mainline approach for inducing conservation behavior, is appropriate in only one of the four situations associated with nonadoption. In reality, these four reasons for nonadoption are not mutually exclusive. Two or more of these circumstances often work together to reinforce reasons for nonadoption. Furthermore, research to determine the distribution of landusers among these four categories has been lacking. But getting conservation district and agency representatives to recognize that diversity exists in the reasons for nonadoption is a critical first step in making local implementation processes more effective. Somehow we need to begin to lose that limited mentality that emphasizes only one policy feature (e.g., voluntary cost-sharing *or* cross-compliance *or* regulation) and begin to recognize that local conservationists need the flexibility to respond with a full range of policy options.

Evaluating implementation efforts. Another strategy to address our current implementation dilemma is to institute an objective evaluation process. One of the frustrations of attempting to analyze implementation processes is that we have little data on this topic. We know it is important, but most of our data are based on anecdotal information or informal observation. The simple fact of the matter is that we do not know when, where, or why implementation is successful or unsuccessful. Success or failure has traditionally been attributed to the design of the conservation policy. This situation can be changed by beginning to measure implementation processes at local and state levels.

Physical data, such as an erosion vulnerability index, can be used to assess where implementation is needed versus where it is actually occurring. Rather than just measuring tons of soil saved or dollars spent per ton of soil saved, we also need a relative measure. That is a measure of the erosion rate on the now-protected field relative to the distribution of erosion rates within the jurisdictional boundaries. Rather than emphasizing the overall amount of conservation applied, this would focus on *where* it is applied. This would determine the distribution of conservation resources being allocated relative to the distribution of excessive erosion within the local jurisdictional unit. The expectation would be that a certain proportion of critical areas, however they may be defined, would be brought under a conservation system on a periodic basis. Quotas established by the district would be determined by the amount of critical area within its boundaries relative to personnel, cost-sharing, and educational resources available. Formulating standards to insure that realistic quotas were established by each conservation district would be a responsibility of the state association of conservation districts.

Initially, conservation districts would be responsible for conducting a needs assessment with landusers to determine the perceived or real reasons for nonadoption (Figure 2) of conservation practices on the identified critical areas. Conservation districts would then create annual plans of work that would specify the responsibility of each agency in meeting the identified needs and specified quota. The ASCS county committee would be informed about where the concentration of cost-sharing funds would be needed; SCS on where and what types of practices should be emphasized, based on available cost-sharing and educational assistance; and CES on where to locate demonstration projects of the selected practices as well as other types of needed educational activities. These efforts would be coordinated with any state or local programs supervised by the conservation district.

The conservation district in conjunction with the state association would be responsible for monitoring the implementation of these annual plans. The major purpose of annual meetings of state associations would be to report publicly on the extent to which the established quotas have been achieved in each district. This public ranking would serve three purposes. First, it would facilitate the identification of common obstacles among the conservation districts relative to the implementation of conservation programs. If need assessments were conducted in all districts and if agency responsibilities were specified in district plans, then obstacles other than those due to the design of the policy would begin to emerge. This would negate the common rationalization "if we only had more money..." and begin to focus on what is being done with existing funds. The common obstacles identified would begin to include the relationships among conservation agencies as well as the nature of their relations with landusers.

Second, the public reporting of district efforts in meeting established quotas would assist the watchdog role of nonagricultural groups that would have vested interests in the implementation of conservation policy. An objective of conservation policies is to protect the public interest. Therefore, reporting on the effectiveness of policy implementation should facilitate greater public awareness and debate. This will serve to strengthen support for effective efforts while focusing constructive criticism on the causes of ineffective efforts.

Third, this annual evaluation of implementation efforts would assist conservation agency administrators in managing their organizations. This would be crucial as conservation agencies would be evaluated on the basis of where the conservation treatments were applied rather than the overall amount of land protected. Obstacles associated with interorganizational communication and coordination would emerge in this process. This, in turn, would provide guidance for future training of personnel. The conservation district need assessments would identify program areas requiring additional research or support resources. Problems that continue to emerge through several planning cycles could be the basis for transfers or lower personnel evaluations. Finally, the results of these planning and evaluation cycles could be used by regional or national agency administrators in designing future program administrative rules, distributing resources to address targeted areas, and the formulation of interagency agreements.

This can be recognized as a proposal for cross-compliance to be applied to the organizations that work with landusers. Although many of the details would have to be worked out, with the above suggestions only meant to broach the idea, it could be argued that this is a logical response to the current situation. If many landusers are not adopting conservation because of the lack of actions, or inappropriate actions by the conservation organizations, then why should the penalty (conservation compliance or the continued degradation of the land resource) only be oriented to the landuser? Or to borrow a phrase from the social science literature, perhaps it is time we stopped blaming the victim (the landuser) and began to focus our attention on other causes for continued resource degradation. These other causes are found among the organizations responsible for implementing conservation policy.

Conclusion

Implementation processes have enormous influence on the effectiveness of conservation policies. Understanding this influence must be based on diagnosis of interorganizational and organization-landuser relations. The limited research in this area leads one to conclude that past policy ineffectiveness may have had more to do with the nature of these relations than with the nature of the policy itself.

Among the strategies available to improve current implementation processes are the following: enhance the leadership capacity of the conservation districts, increase awareness of a need for diverse policy tools to match the diversity found in the reasons for nonadoption of conservation practices, and evaluation of implementation efforts.

Implementation is largely a political process. For this reason it is understandable why so little attention has been focused on implementating conservation policy. It is far safer to analyze politically passive situations, such as degradation processes or features of ideal policy in a perfect market, than it is to investigate the faults of fellow conservation actors. It is also safer in an era of budget retrenchment to look for new policy directions than to analyze and respond to past deficiencies. This quick fix mentality has always been a more attractive political option than specifying administrative or leadership mediocrity. Yet maintaining the false assumption that implementation is occuring in an effective manner has been a consequence of all these ''safe'' decisions, an assumption we no longer can afford to maintain.

REFERENCES

1. Bardach, E. 1977. *The implementation game: What happens after a bill becomes law.* MIT Press, Cambridge, Massachusetts.
2. Bultena, G., E. Hoiberg, and P. Nowak. 1984. *Sources of conservation informa-*

tion and participation in conservation programs: An interregional analysis. Sociological Studies of Environmental Issues, Report 156. Department of Sociology and Anthropology, Iowa State University, Ames.

3. DeCoursey, D. G. 1985. *Mathematical models for nonpoint water pollution control.* Journal of Soil and Water Conservation 40(5): 408-413.

4. Gianessi, L., H. Peskin, P. Crosson, and C. Puffer. 1986. *Nonpoint-source pollution: Are cropland controls the answer.* Journal of Soil and Water Conservation 41(4): 215-218.

5. Gillette, D. 1986. *Wind erosion.* In *Soil Conservation: Assessing the National Resource Inventory.* Volume 2. National Academy Press, Washington, D.C.

6. Griswold, J. 1987. *Assessment and planning staff report: Assessment report of the conservation credit pilot project.* Soil Conservation Service, U.S. Department of Agriculture, Washington, D.C.

7. Hoban, T., P. Korsching, and T. Huffman. 1986. *The selling of soil conservation: A test of the voluntary approach, volume 2: Organizational survey.* Sociological Studies of Environmental Issues, Report 158. Department of Sociology and Anthropology, Iowa State University, Ames.

8. Hoover, H., and M. Wiitala. 1980. *Operator and landlord participation in soil erosion control in the Maple Creek watershed in northeast Nebraska.* Staff Report National Resources Economics Division 80-4. Economics Research Service, U.S. Department of Agriculture, Washington, D.C.

9. Larson, W., T. Fenton, E. Skidmore, and C. Benbrook. 1985. *Effects of soil erosion on soil properties as related to crop productivity and classification.* In R. Follett and B. Steward [editors] *Soil Erosion and Crop Productivity.* American Society of Agronomy, Madison, Wisconsin.

10. Leman, C. 1982. *Political dilemmas in evaluating and budgeting soil conservation programs: The RCA process.* In H. Halcrow, E. Heady, M. Cotner [editors] *Soil Conservation Policies, Institutions and Incentives.* Soil Conservation Society of America, Ankeny, Iowa.

11. National Research Council. 1986. *Soil conservation: Assessing the National Resources Inventory.* Volume 1. National Academy Press, Washington, D.C.

12. Neuschatz, A. 1973. *Managing the environment.* EPA-600/5-73-010. U.S. Environmental Protection Agency, Washington, D.C.

13. Nielson, J. 1986. *Conservation targeting: Success or failure?* Journal of Soil and Water Conservation 41(2): 70-76.

14. Nowak, P. 1984. *Adoption and diffusion of soil and water conservation practices.* In B. English, J. Maetzold, B. Holding, and E. Heady [editors] *Future Agricultural Technology and Resource Conservation.* Iowa State University Press, Ames.

15. Nowak, P. 1985. *The leadership crisis in conservation districts.* Journal of Soil and Water Conservation 40(5): 421-425.

16. Nowak, P. 1986. *Farmer's opinions about soil and water conservation issues.* Minnesota Soil and Water Conservation Board, St. Paul.

17. Pierce F., W. Larson, R. Dowdy, and W. Graham. 1983. *Productivity of soils: Assessing long-term changes due to erosion.* Journal of Soil and Water Conservation 38(1): 39-44.

18. Potter, H., and H. Schweer. 1984. *Interorganizational relations and decision making among section 208 water quality management planning agencies.* Water Resources Research Center Technical Report 165. Purdue University, West Lafayette, Indiana.

19. Pressman, J., and A. Wildavsky. 1973. *Implementation.* University of California Press, Berkeley.

20. Rogers, E. 1983. *Diffusions of Innovations.* The Free Press, New York, New York.

21. Rogers, D., and M. Maas. 1977. *Interagency planning for natural resource management.* Report 137. Department of Sociology and Anthropology, Iowa State University, Ames.

22. Runge, C. F., W. Larson, and G. Roloff. 1986. *A Midwestern perspective on targeting conservation programs to protect soil productivity.* In *Soil Conservation: Assessing the National Resources Inventory.* Volume 2. National Academy Press, Washington, D.C.

23. Sampson, N. 1985. *For love of the land: A history of the national associaton of conservation districts.* National Association of Conservation Districts, League City, Texas.

24. Walker, D., and D. Young. 1986. *Assessing soil erosion productivity damage.* In *Soil Conservation: Assessing the National Resources Inventory.* Volume 2. National Academy Press, Washington, D.C.

25. Williams, J., and K. Renard. 1985. *Assessments of soil erosion and crop productivity with process models (EPIC).* In R. Follett and B. Steward [editors] *Soil Erosion and Crop Productivity.* American Society of Agronomy, Madison, Wisconsin.

26. Williams, J., K. Renard, and P. Dyke. 1983. *EPIC: A new method for assessing erosion's effect on soil productivity.* Journal of Soil and Water Conservation 38(5): 381-383.

II

Federal soil and water conservation policy

5

Intergovernmental relations and soil and water conservation

Norman A. Berg

Soil and water conservation programs forged over the past 50 years need to confront and overcome longstanding flaws and limitations if they are to deal effectively with current-day and future soil and water conservation issues.

The nation continues to have a serious soil erosion problem. At least 69 million acres of cropland were eligible for the first three U.S. Department of Agriculture signups for the new Conservation Reserve Program. These soils were classified as "highly erodible" at the 3T (three times tolerance) erosion level. Interim rules for the other provisions of the Food Security Act of 1985 (the sodbuster and conservation compliance phases) establish a definition for eligible soils (erodibility index) that encompasses nearly 118 million cropland acres.

Excessive soil erosion persists in the United States despite a substantial effort at all levels of government to support the most scientifically advanced and best funded soil and water conservation program in the history of civilization. There are many good stewards of the land, and there are many excellent showcases of conservation progress. However, too many land-users, focusing on the short-term as they attempt to survive in today's institutional and economic climate, are forced to produce rather than protect.

During my tenure at the Soil Conservation Service, soil conservation programs had some good years. There were crop rotations, contoured farms, stripcropping as far as they eye could see, terraces, windbreaks, wildlife plantings and ponds, and a host of site-specific conservation practices applied to the land. Voluntary conservation district programs, coupled with government-funded research, extension, financial, and technical assistance programs, proved adequate to achieve good conservation and resource managment systems on millions of acres of farmland. But those years are history. Agriculture has now, for more than a decade, been challenged with change. Farms and fields are bigger and crop rotations are gone, along with old fencerows. Straight-row corn and soybean farming dominates.

An overdue assessment

The Soil and Water Resources Conservation Act of 1977, vetoed earlier by President Gerald Ford as a federal land use planning threat, was a deliberate effort of some scope and magnitude, to review soil and water conservation programs within USDA and make recommendations for improvement. It was recognized that the "fencerow-to-fencerow" thrust in American agriculture had damaged the resource base. The 1977 National Resources Inventory, an overdue activity, produced reliable data on conditions and trends regarding the nonfederal resource landscape and was used extensively.

RCA and NRI accomplished two purposes. The general public was again made aware of the soil, water, and other renewable natural resource problems that persisted, in spite of the government conservation programs enacted since the 1930s. Second, the data and further studies revealed that a large share of the nation's soil loss is associated with a relatively small proportion of the land. This observation was found to be true of the major types of erosion—wind, sheet, and rill—and of all land uses (cropland, rangeland, pasture, and forest). This was not the type of information that some states and many local governments (conservation districts) wanted to hear. Although all states and most farms have soil erosion, local concern for shifting limited resources to priority areas precluded USDA from making significant program changes. The NRI data and other timely information and conditions, including surplus supplies of corn, wheat, and cotton, however, did provide a rationale for the Conservation Reserve.

In 1977 about 38 million acres of nonirrigated cropland—11 percent of the total—was eroding in excess of 15 tons per acre per year— accounting for 1.3 billion tons of soil erosion. This was about 53 percent of the total sheet, rill, and wind erosion on nonirrigated cropland. Taken alone, sheet and rill erosion, the most serious forms of soil loss on U.S. cropland, were even more concentrated. In 1977, 25 million acres, about 6 percent of total cropland, accounted for 43 percent of the total tonnage of cropland sheet and rill erosion (828 million tons annually).

Although there are important exceptions, the American Farmland Trust's review of research on erosion's effects on soil productivity and off-site damages being done in the U.S. is associated with land experiencing high rates of soil loss. Typically, those rates exceed the national average soil loss by a factor of three or more. A further observation by AFT was that the highly erodible land, accounting for much of the cropland erosion problem, appeared to be eluding most methods of conservation farming, as well as the services of traditional USDA conservation programs. Therefore, as the debate and discussion generated by the NRIs, the RCA process, and the pending 1985 farm bill grew in intensity, a conservation coalition emerged to speak for a variety of special interest conservation and environmental publics. These national nonprofit organizations, representing wildlife, forestry, land use, water quality, range, conservation districts, and even state and local governments, were determined to improve "farm policy."

New initiatives

Several states, including Minnesota, Wisconsin, Illinois, Iowa, Missouri, South Dakota, and Nebraska, have in recent years moved ahead of the federal government with many soil and water conservation initiatives. Illinois has its plan creating a workable guideline to achieve a tolerable soil loss level, T by 2000. Minnesota has its outstanding Reinvest in Minnesota effort underway.

The American Farmland Trust conducted an independent analysis of soil conservation programs (1982-1984). This study "Soil Conservation in America—What Do We Have To Lose?" took advantage of an opportunity to involve those people too often left out of policy debates—the farmers themselves. The 23 recommendations of that report included the conservation reserve and sodbuster features of the 1985 farm bill and indicated strong support for conservation compliance. The foundation was laid for the linkage of conservation and commodity policies in USDA, and a later AFT report, "Future Policy Directions for American Agriculture," outlined an integrated conservation-commodity option. The impacts of the policy changes discussed in that report were measured in the context of industry performance—production, consumption, and prices.

The U.S. House of Representatives, during the 98th Congress, incorporated several conservation provisions into a measure that passed. That measure was opposed, however, by the administration (except for a weak sodbuster feature that had passed the Senate). The conferees were not able to reach agreement because the Senate position was to delay action until consideration of the 1985 farm bill in the 99th Congress.

Senator Roger Jepsen of Iowa, with excellent staff assistance from Karla Perri, had led several activities that were to be of great value even after his election loss to Senator Tom Harkin. Senator Jepsen established an advisory committee, composed of most of the members of the conservation coalition. This group met several times to examine the 1981 farm bill and to recommend legislative language for possible use during the pending debate on the bill. The intent was to be prepared for any windows of opportunity to link commodity and conservation policy in the 99th Congress. Senator Jepsen also chaired a conservation subcommittee for the Senate Committee on Agriculture, Nutrition, and Forestry and was the chairman of the Joint Economic Committee. This committee held extensive hearings in June 1983. However, the circumstances for action had not yet come together. The massive, temporary cropland use adjustment and the substantial federal cost of the payment-in-kind (PIK) program in 1983 was to eventually prove of limited value to conservation. That activity did add reasons for a long-term land use adjustment.

A window of opportunity

The Ninety-Ninth Congress, First Session, turned out to be that long-sought window of opportunity. On April 15, 1985, Senator Richard G. Lugar of Indiana convened a hearing on "Conservation and Extension Issues." Governor John Evans of Idaho was the first witness, and 17 leaders of national organizations followed. Their testimony that eventful morning was impressive. The mix of interests represented by the witnesses included forestry, soil conservation, fish and wildlife, environmental concerns, water quality, farm organizations, professional societies, and state and local governments.

It is reported that Senator Lugar, at the conclusion of the hearing, instructed his staff to begin drafting the legislation that would eventually become the conservation title of the 1985 farm bill. This would be a bipartisan effort and a great deal of prior work, including the legislation that had passed the House of Representatives in the 98th Congress, would prove valuable.

As the Senate Committee on Agriculture, Nutrition, and Forestry moved ahead on its legislation, the House Committee on Agriculture resumed its work on a version of conservation legislation. That committee had longstanding bipartisan support and had conducted several hearings that indicated strong support for their actions.

The administration, earlier in the year, had sent Congress a market-oriented version of farm policy. The only conservation provision was a weak version of the sodbuster concept. We were told that the secretary of agriculture supported a conservation reserve but could not get approval for a reserve from the Office of Management and Budget. After it was clear that Congress would include a comprehensive conservation title, the administration allowed the secretary to hold a historic news conference. In June 1985, accompanied by Senator Lugar on an Indiana farm, the secretary announced support for a 20-million acre, 10-year, $11 billion Conservation Reserve Program.

His announcement reversed the stand reflected in USDA testimony two months earlier at a House Subcommittee on Conservation, Credit, and Rural Development. That testimony, while supporting the concept of reducing federal incentives that contribute to cultivation of fragile soils (sodbuster) and urging greater consistency in USDA farm and conservation programs, made no reference to swampbuster or conservation compliance. In closing comments, a USDA witness said, ''Mr. Chairman, at this point in my testimony I would like to respond briefly to your letter of March 26, in which you requested that we provide information about studies and analysis of a conservation reserve. USDA economists have done research in this area, of which two examples are: a paper by Dr. Roy M. Gray of the Soil Conservation Service entitled; 'Long-Term Conservation Reserve for Highly Erodible and Seriously Eroding Lands,' and a paper by the Economic Research Service entitled, 'Analysis of Policies to Conserve Soil and Reduce Surplus Crop Production'.''

The conservation coalition monitored all aspects of the work in Congress relating to conservation, credit, and farmland protection. On December 23, 1985, the President signed Public Law 99-198. Title XII—Conservation—was held up as a landmark decision (Figure 1).

A new approach to conservation

The Food Security Act of 1985 fundamentally changes the nation's approach to resource conservation. It explicitly incorporates consistent environmental and economic (commodity) program objectives. The CRP has the potential to include 87 percent of the nation's most threatened cropland

and to reduce soil erosion substantially. At the same time, the program can assist in reducing the substantial excess production capacity that has emerged in agriculture in recent years. The new CRP also has operating features that are market-oriented. Individual farmer bids are used to determine the economic incentive needed to conserve soil resources. This approach must be monitored.

Progress at the federal level is most commendable in achieving a limited linkage of commodity and conservation policies in the farm bill of 1985. Who would have believed a year ago that USDA would be letting farmers bid to retire their most highly erodible croplands to grass, trees, or wildlife cover? Who would have predicted nearly 9 million acres of Conservation Reserve contracts in a 10-year obligation? Who would have forecast that sodbuster, swampbuster, conservation compliance, and conservation easements provisions of the Food Security Act of 1985 would be implemented by the USDA and others? Who would have been confident that Title XII of Public Law 99-198 would be, a year later, one of the least controversial features of the new law? Finally, who would have thought that policymakers (Congress and the administration) and conservationists could capitalize on a historic turning point in agricultural resource policy? The recently available information about erosion in the U.S. (the 1977 and 1982 National Resources Inventories), the outlook for the farm economy, the policy environment in Washington, strong support for conservation (RCA), and the debate over farm policy (that it wasn't working) all coincided to make 1984, 1985, and 1986 critical years in the history of soil conservation policy. We didn't achieve every item needing action, but the federal government is now, for the first time in my experience, on record as favoring good land use and rewarding good stewardship by removing the incentives to crop highly erodible lands or valuable wetlands.

The states and local governments should find this action encouraging and more conducive to harmonious working relations. The federal government, carrying as it has for 50 years the majority of the funding for conservation, is now sending a strong signal that this could and should change. It has done this in several ways. First, USDA farm programs will not be readily available to those who ignore certain soil and water conservation requirements. Those who have land that is now grass or trees—and would be highly erodible if converted to cropland—must have an approved conservation plan from their local conservation district to continue to receive farm program benefits. The sodbuster legislation, long needed, is now a law of the land and should have broad support for implementation. Highly erodible cropland that is not bid into the CRP and requires a conservation

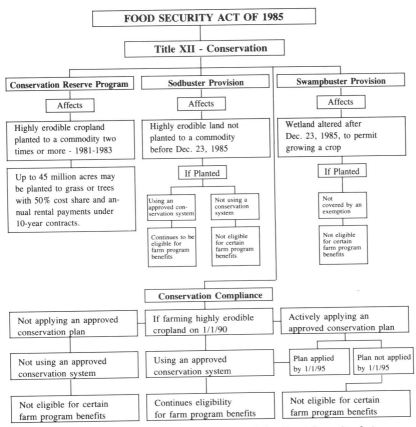

Figure 1. Provisions in the conservation title of the Food Security Act.

plan by 1990 and implementation of that plan by 1995 to qualify for farm program benefits has an exception: if soil survey is needed, there is a two-year delay while that is completed.

Any land considered wetland, by a set of technical definitions, would, if converted to cropland after December 23, 1985, be denied farm program benefits. The conservation plan escape mechanism (of the sodbuster and conservation compliance provisions) does not apply to this feature of the law. Land determined to have been drained, dredged, filled, leveled, or otherwise manipulated for the purpose, or to have the effect of making the production of an agricultural commodity possible, would be denied farm program benefits if one or more of the hydric soils criteria of such wetland have been removed or if the hydrophytic vegetation on such wetland has been removed or destroyed.

Obviously, landowners and users can still decide how to use the land, providing they do not violate a nonfederal law and do *not* want to qualify for several USDA programs as spelled out in the interim rules issued June 27, 1986, in the *Federal Register.*

As the potential impacts of sodbuster, swampbuster, and conservation compliance are more fully realized at the farm and ranch level, opposition to implementation will probably surface. The swampbuster and conservation compliance features are most vulnerable as implementation accelerates.

The first two signups for the CRP have shown the potential for reducing soil erosion. USDA has analyzed the data by states, and the soil saved annually is significant. The erosion rate on the first 828,383 acres accepted ranged from 4.8 tons per acre per year in Alaska to 56.9 tons per acre per year in New Jersey. The average for the U.S. was 29.65 tons per acre per year. Total annual erosion exceeded 24 million tons. The estimated soil to be saved annually surpasses 21.5 million tons.

The soil erosion rate of the first *and second* 3,824,566 acres accepted in contracts ranged from 3.9 tons per acre per year in Alaska to 56 tons per acre per year in Oklahoma. The average for the U.S. was 30.7 tons per acre per year. The total annual erosion was nearly 115 million tons. Assuming erosion at 3 tons per acre per year remaining after establishment of permanent vegetation, the estimated reduction is nearly 106 million tons per year.

The third signup of 5,091,618 CRP acres could, assuming an average soil erosion rate of 29 tons per acre per year, save another 145 million tons of soil each year. The estimated 2.5 billion tons of CRP-reduced soil erosion, over 10 years at a total rental cost of $4 billion, indicates a cost per ton of soil saved of less than $2. This does not include cost-sharing. The total costs would be partially offset by savings generated by lower farm program costs.

USDA has estimated that when the CRP is fully implemented 764 million tons of erosion will be controlled each year. The average cost of the earlier 20-million-acre, $11-billion CRP would have been about $55.00 per acre per year. Annual costs for the first three signups averaged about $45.00 per acre. Average costs per acre will probably increase and soil loss reduction per acre decrease as the total CRP acreage builds toward the 45-million-acre goal. Only two of the 133 pools nationwide are now accepting bids at the maximum rate ($90.00 per acre per year). These are in Illinois and Iowa. A Minnesota pool has the lowest maximum acceptable rate ($20.00

per acre per year). After the first round of bids (March 1986), landowners became more realistic in their bidding. There was no precedent for bidding during the first signup period. Bids in March varied widely, and only 15 percent were accepted. A farmer in one state, where land values traditionally had been high, offered to retire his land for $700 per acre per year. Other bids were as low as $5 per acre per year. During the second signup period in May, bidding was more consistent. More than 67 percent of the bids were accepted. In the August signup 35,965 of the 45,081 bids were accepted. Across the U.S., the response has been as varied as the land.

After three signups, the accepted CRP acreage in the 10 highest states was as follows: Texas, 1,137,000 acres; Colorado, 1,132,000 acres; Minnesota, 662,000 acres; Kansas, 618,000 acres; Oklahoma, 441,000 acres; New Mexico, 421,000 acres; Iowa, 358,000; Montana, 354,000 acres; Missouri, 353,000 acres; Oregon, 322,000 acres.

So far, 69,135 CRP contracts (8,930,655 acres) have resulted from 123,718 bids (15,886,049 acres). Although data are available from only the first signup, the largest acreage involved wheat, followed by corn, oats, and sorghum. The average base reduction was about one-half the total CRP acreage. The average yield reduction was also calculated for each crop, but these data need further analysis.

The American Farmland Trust, through a contract with Professor J.D. Esseks of Northern Illinois University, is now analyzing the results of telephone interviews with nearly 1,200 cropland owners in 61 counties from 23 states. Soil Conservation Service NRI data were used to select sample counties with a very high percentage of highly erodible cropland. Agricultural Stabilization and Conservation Service records were used to select the farmers to be interviewed. CRP bidders and nonbidders were contacted. The objective was to find out what works and what does not work in securing acceptable contracts. This information is being provided to members of Congress, the administration, and the conservation coalition to improve the CRP.

What problems ahead?

What are the problems to be solved for full implementation of all the provisions of the Conservation Title of Public Law 99-198?

Conservation Reserve Program. Final rules for this activity should be issued as soon as possible. The definition of highly erodible land should be consistent with that used to administer the sodbuster and conservation compliance provisions of the farm bill.

The key feature of the new law, CRP, is the only provision that requires a commitment of federal funds. Acceptance of bids for CRP contracts depends upon USDA having the ability to guarantee funds for 10-year rental payments. After the 1987 crop year, based on the present law, the ability to use the Commodity Credit Corporation for these purposes will expire. The future of the CRP will depend upon direct appropriations beginning in fiscal year 1988. This will be difficult because of many factors, including efforts by OMB to reduce USDA conservation expenditures.

Another challenge will be—if funds are available—to attract bidders willing to contract up to 45 million acres of highly erodible cropland at reasonable rental rates by 1991.

Finally, the objectives of CRP can be achieved only when the acres converted to grass, trees, and wildlife cover are made permanent. The nonuse restriction on those lands is unwise. The cost of bidding is higher, the cost of maintaining the proper cover is increased, and the potential for that land to return to cropland use at the expiration of the contract is increased. This feature of CRP should be changed.

Sodbuster. This provision of the law, as a disincentive, has broad support and should be closly monitored for compliance. The final rules will be most important for long-term implementation. Cropping on these lands will depend upon applying a locally approved conservation plan.

Swampbuster. There are already suggestions that this provision not be implemented. Final rules will be significant in several ways, including the means of deciding when (before December 23, 1985) and how (was it a natural condition?) the conversion of properly defined wetlands would be exempt.

Conservation compliance. This is the most demanding provision of the law. After 1989 all highly erodible cropland not in the CRP and still cropped using USDA farm programs will be subject to requirements of a locally approved conservation plan. If an erodibility index of 8 is used, USDA could have to write conservation plans for about 118 million acres.

Traditional conservation programs of USDA

The House of Representatives, when reporting the Agriculture, Rural Development, and Related Agencies Appropriation Bill for fiscal year 1987, reminded the administration of its conservation priorities. H.R.5177, along with Report 99-686, restored $432,448,000 of proposed conservation program budget reductions or eliminations. The budget recommendations for several years have attempted to severely limit USDA spending for several activities. These include the Agricultural Conservation Program, the Watershed Protection and Flood Prevention Program (P.L.566 and P.L.534), the Great Plains Conservation Program, the Resource Conservation and Development Program, River Basin Surveys and Investigations, the Water Bank, and the Forestry Incentives Program. In addition, the Congress made certain that extension, research, and credit dedicated to soil and water conservation would be not be impaired. A congressional report said, "A review of the contributions that the conservation programs have made to the protection and preservation of the country's basic resources and its ability to produce plentiful supplies of wholesome and inexpensive food for domestic and overseas consumers clearly shows their great value to the Nation."

Also, in the interest of continued long-term conservation of the nation's basic resources, the report went on to state, *"It is essential that the new Conservation Reserve Program not be used to replace existing conservation programs.* The programs which have been in operation during the past 50 years have served this country well. They should not be discontinued or severely curtailed. *The new program should add to, not replace, the existing time-proven programs."*

To make certain the administration was listening, the House Committee, with the cooperation of Congress, included a provision in the Supplemental Appropriations Act (P.L.99-263) which should accomplish "the objectives outlined above." The committee also cautioned that, "in carrying out the new CRP, it is essential that sign-up agreements not reduce total production below levels needed to meet domestic needs, maintain the supply line, and provide an adequate supply for export at competitive prices either by the Commodity Credit Corporation or by private traders. It is essential to future economic health of agriculture and the country that a policy of ample production rather than scarcity be followed."

Therefore, the annual federal conservation programs of USDA will probably continue to expend about $1 billion. Spending by nonfederal governments has gradually moved upward. The actual contributions reached a high of $357 million in 1984; 1985 actual contributions were down 3.5 percent from 1984; but 1986 appropriations show a 4 percent increase in state and local contributions over the 1985 appropriations. This trend will be encouraged, as the administration seeks to "privatize" the work.

6

Trends in federal soil and water conservation policy

Charles M. Benbrook

Soil and water conservation policy tops the list of encouraging developments in the agricultural arena, although that list is indeed a short one. Some analysts have been critical of the progress made to date in implementing the Conservation Reserve Program—too critical in my view. Surely some tough problems stand in the way of expanding CRP enrollment in feedgrain producing areas. But there is nothing wrong with the CRP concept. With some 9 million acres and 60,000 farmers already enrolled, the program has thus far been a tremendous success. It is ready to deliver on some very big promises.

Within two years more than 60 million acres could be enrolled in the CRP, of which 5 million could be enrolled under special, targeted state and federal programs designed to address water quality and quantity problems.

The focus here on information and administrative issues is timely. Solid, reliable, nationally consistent information, used in a practical and fair administrative process, is a necessary condition for the CRP to work as intended. The two other essential ingredients—common sense and wisdom in the political and budgetary arenas—are sometimes harder to come by. But so far so good.

Early in 1987 the 100th Congress will be forced to review the projected cost overruns of the commodity programs. Presumably, steps will have to be taken to reduce the cost of these programs by about one-third, bringing projected costs down from about $25 billion to about $18 billion, the amount provided in the fiscal year 1987 appropriation bill. Alternatively, Congress could pass a supplemental appropriation to cover the cost overrun—a not-too-likely prospect.

Assuming program costs are trimmed, the economic attractiveness of the commodity programs will be somewhat reduced relative to enrollment in the CRP. While some steps are likely to cut costs, Congress no doubt will take other, new steps to address persistent surplus and income problems. In all likelihood an effort will be made to retire more acreage in 1987 than now called for in the Food Security Act of 1985. As I perceive the political landscape, the only two viable options are a paid diversion or accelerating enrollment in the CRP. Because of budget considerations, the CRP option could emerge as the preferred course of action. But the question remains—are we really ready to enroll perhaps 35 million additional acres in the CRP in the next six months? The answer will be determined by how well the policy community deals with several critical issues.

Critical and pressing issues

Five issues seem most critical to me at this point:

1. *The size of the eligible pool for CRP enrollment as set by the definition of highly erodible land.* Persuasive arguments can and have been made for keeping the pool of eligible cropland small relative to CRP enrollments. In recent months support has grown somewhat for enlarging the pool as a step toward encouraging more competitive bidding and greater enrollments. I question the logic and analysis underlying the notion that expanding the pool of eligible land will bring down bids because such an expansion would involve more productive land likely to bring somewhat higher acreage rental rates. Notwithstanding uncertainty about this point, the one and only really good reason to expand the pool is expanding the target and rate of CRP enrollment. If the U.S. Department of Agriculture and Congress make a firm commitment to enrolling 20 million acres or more in the next 12 months, I would not argue against definition of highly erodible land based on an erodibility index of 8 or higher (EI ≥ 8). Such a definition is attractive on other grounds:

▶ It ensures consistency with the conservation compliance and the sodbuster provisions, thereby greatly diminishing future administrative hassles, costs, and challenges.

▶ It is based on the most technically defensible concept for the classification of cropland with respect to inherent erodibility and vulnerability to erosion-induced productivity damages.

▶ The definition can readily accommodate improved universal soil loss equation data on expected erosion rates, or more accurate T values based on new data and models involving erosion-productivity impacts. Such improved data could be generated and incorporated in an EI-based definition at the state or national level.

If such a commitment to expand the CRP fails to materialize, highly erodible land should be restricted to cultivated cropland now eroding at more than twice the soil loss tolerance limit, with $EI \geq 8$. This definition yields a pool of about 65 million acres.

2. *Achieving a more even pattern of CRP enrollment.* The CRP has proved particularly popular in arid regions growing cotton, sorghum, and wheat and small grains. It is easy to understand why: CRP rental rates have approached or exceeded cash rental rates. Moreover, enrollees receive their CRP payments every year without the need to summerfallow.

The reason acceptable bid levels reached a level above cash rents in some areas can be explained by looking at USDA's formula for setting maximum accepted bid levels. Cash rental rates are the dominant factor used within a pool in setting maximum acceptable bids. The rent on dryland acres is averaged with the much higher rent on irrigated land in regions with both types of cropland. As a result, USDA allows dryland acreage to enter the reserve at unnecessarily inflated prices. This problem is surfacing in Texas, the West, and the Great Plains.

To get the economics right in the Midwest, the economic attractiveness of reserve enrollment must rise relative to participation in the feedgrain program. This will not happen by natural processes and is the most worrisome issue standing in the way of rapid expansion of CRP enrollments.

3. *Commodity program-CRP interactions: Is competition inevitable?* The answer is no. Without important program reforms, the answer is yes. Clearly, a balanced approach will involve steps to reduce somewhat the economic attractiveness of the commodity programs, while increasing somewhat the lure of the CRP. Possible and improbable steps toward the first goal are outlined below:

▶ Continue to require maximum acreage set-asides allowed in law (20 percent for the feedgrain program), or even increase percentage set-asides.

▶ Driven by budgetary concerns, the Congress may choose to reduce the corn support price to about $1.75, a step that will also be credited with making U.S. commodities more competitive in international markets. At the same time, target prices would also be cut back somewhat more on a percentage basis, to perhaps about $2.50. Deficiency payments would, as a result, fall to perhaps 75 cents per bushel, from about $1.20. Politically, a 53-cent reduction in the corn target price will prove extremely unpalatable, despite the more than $2 billion in probable savings. Compared with the alternatives though, such a drastic step could emerge as the only course of action that can gain the support of a majority in Congress. Similar changes would probably be adopted in other commodity programs.

▶ Impose and enforce much stricter payment limitation provisions in conjunction with a higher, more realistic cap on payments.

▶ As suggested by Taft and Runge, forbid the use of highly erodible land in satisfying set-aside requirements. While novel, this idea could have adverse consequences in areas where a high percentage of land meets the definition of highly erodible. It could compel farmers to plant program crops on highly erodible land, while setting aside better cropland. This idea will also require considerable oratorical skills when brought before the Committee on Agriculture.

▶ Strictly monitor established yields and base acreage to ensure no increases are allowed in either.

▶ Require cross-compliance—farmers enrolling in one commodity program (say wheat) must comply with the pertinent provisions of other programs (feedgrains) on all farms operated by them.

▶ Adopt program changes that impose equal costs of program participation in areas where acreage is summerfallowed in alternate years, in contrast to regions where continuous cropping patterns are used.

4. *Increasing the attractiveness of CRP enrollment for highly erodible cropland also eligible for commodity program participation.* The most direct approach would be to raise the acceptable bid levels in pools with a relatively high portion of commodity program base acres. Because of budget exposure, this option may be among the last given serious consideration and can only be evaluated in terms of net costs once the provisions of the 1987 commodity programs are fully specified. Indeed, higher acceptable bid levels may prove the cheapest alternative to achieve more ambitious 1987 production adjustment goals. The scuttlebut in the halls of USDA on a paid diversion is that a payment on the order of $1.75 to $2.00 per bushel of corn base yield could be required. Such a rich offer would surely have a profound and negative impact on CRP enrollment.

It would also be possible to modify or eliminate the provision in the CRP that reduces a farm's base acres proportional to CRP enrollment. Because such a change would undercut an important aspect of the supply control benefits of the CRP, this option is not likely to be favorably received, though it makes sense if the only goal is to increase CRP enrollment.

Another approach would be to convince farmers that the projected 10-year benefit stream from traditional commodity programs will shrink if the Congress gets serious about budget deficits. Without a cut next year in target prices though, farmers are not likely to take seriously the notion that program benefits are vulnerable politically.

Steps to educate farmers about the consequences in 1990 of conservation compliance could be initiated. This represents a tough task, however, because it will remain inherently unclear in many regions of the country just what the consequences will be, at least until the definition of highly erodible land and many other administrative program requirements are settled.

Several other program reforms merit consideration if a serious effort is made to accelerate CRP enrollment.

► Move toward larger substate bidding pools to allow greater flexibility and choice within pools.

► Raise the 25 percent cap on CRP acreage enrollment in a county to 50 percent.

► Allow in some states, where adverse affects on the cattle industry can be avoided, the use of CRP lands for haying and grazing in addition to forestry uses. This option is attractive on budgetary grounds because average acceptable bids would probably fall $20 to $30 per acre if haying or grazing were allowed. A recent survey by the American Farmland Trust of farmers considering enrollment in the CRP indentified the prohibition against economic use as the most common concern keeping farmers from enrolling more land.

► For farmers in serious financial trouble, allow upfront payment of CRP benefits for debt retirement as part of debt-restructuring agreements.

► Offer farmers bonus payments for giving up base acres in excess of what is required as a condition of CRP enrollment.

5. *Continue to improve the cost-effectiveness of the targeting effort, particularly in the Agricultural Conservation Program.* Steady improvement in the cost-effectiveness of ACP remains an untold conservation success story. This program continues to demonstrate the capacity and willingness to meet emerging needs. To the credit of program adminstrators, problems have been studied and steps have been taken to overcome shortcomings.

These efforts should continue, and deserve greater support. I hope that the Office of Management and Budget will finally recognize and reward USDA for these accomplishments by forgoing the bogus budget savings entailed in zeroing ACP out of the fiscal year 1988 budget. Everyone remotely knowledgeable about this program realizes that the Honorable

Jamie Whitten will restore ACP funds if missing when the budget is submitted to Congress.

Challenges in the field

The conservation title of the farm bill breathes new life into the mission of the Soil Conservation Service and conservation districts. For the first time in decades, programs and policies are in place that provide a realistic set of tools to bring soil erosion largely under control. I think the conservation community is gearing up now and will be able to bear the heavy burdens that will soon fall upon it.

One key to the success of conservation compliance and sodbuster is the timely development of a new generation of farm conservation plans. Because these plans, and compliance with them, will determine eligibility for government program benefits, farmers and conservationists will have to take them far more seriously. Moreover, they will also need to be realistic and flexible, taking into account the special problems faced by certain farmers in some areas.

I must admit some concern about the future of conservation plans in light of new program needs. The type of a plan needed to make sodbuster and conservation compliance administratively viable is very different from the elaborate, whole-farm plans of the past. Yet there remains considerable hesitancy among some to change conservation plans. Problems could arise if SCS is slow to break with tradition. Field personnel will soon become overwhelmed by the workload.

I have another concern. Implementation of sodbuster, swampbuster, and conservation compliance will require clear, strict rules and adherence to them. Yet good judgment and a degree of local flexibility will also be necessary to avoid unnecessary and unjustifiably harsh consequences. For example, suppose cotton producers in the panhandle of Texas can bring erosion rates down from an average of 40 tons per acre to 10 tons, on land with T values of 3 tons. Technically, this would fall short by 4 tons of the 2T goal in conservation compliance.

I do not think it makes sense to, in effect, shut down an operator in situations where 20, 30, or more tons of erosion reduction is agreed upon, yet the 2T goal is missed by a few tons. Nonetheless, it is no easy matter to balance the need for equity across regions in achieving consistent national goals, with a degree of flexibility at the local level. Unless a workable accommodation can be reached between these two critical goals, conservation compliance and sodbuster will remain vulnerable to political and legal challenges.

Similar concerns have arisen in reference to the definition of ''commenced'' in the sodbuster and swampbuster regulations. I think these tricky issues can be resolved in a reasonable, timely way without undermining the integrity of the new conservation provisions or political support for this major new change in direction. At times, antagonists may have to trust each other more than they are accustomed to, but I am convinced common sense can lead to solutions as long as all parties continue to share the goal of conserving our soil and water resources.

There are a host of other, more pragmatic challenges that SCS, the Agricultural Stablization and Conservation Service, and conservation district offices now face. They must:

▶ Identify in the next 24 months what lands meet the definition of ''highly erodible'' and inform landowners and operators associated with these lands.

▶ Greatly simplify the content and process of developing a conservation plan.

▶ Become much more expert in use of the USLE and in understanding from a farmer's perspective the pro and con impacts of various erosion control options.

▶ Systematically explore the potential role of crop rotations as a valuable, often necessary erosion-control practice.

▶ Incorporate water quality concerns and practices into plans.

New directions

I see many important new directions on the horizon that could markedly change how we administer soil and water conservation policy. These include the following:

▶ Senator Sam Nunn is considering introduction of legislation to accelerate the rate of enrollment of land into the CRP and to expand the size of the reserve to 65 million acres. While not a new direction, this legislation suggests a much more immediate and prominent role for the CRP.

▶ A strong case can be made for states assuming a leadership role in initiating water quality and water conservation initiatives in the context of the CRP, conservation compliance, sodbuster, and swampbuster. I see many possibilities and sense that a few key states, including Minnesota, are about ready to move ahead. States might (a) cooperate with SCS in improving the accuracy or adjusting the technical concepts used in identifying highly erodible lands to take water quality concerns into account, (b) demonstrate how to incorporate water quality into conservation plans, and (c) petition USDA to block-grant a portion of CRP funds destined for a state into a special fund to be administered through a targeted federal-state program designed to enroll into the CRP croplands that are irrigated from threatened aquifers (quality or quantity concerns, or both) or that contribute disproportionally to nonpoint pollution problems (either surface or groundwater).

▶ In several parts of the United States, farmers are growing crops that should not be produced and indeed cannot be produced in a profitable manner under current market conditions. These crops, moreover, are often those associated with some of the most blatant abuses of our natural resources. Sound conservation policies—and the flow of dollars associated with the new programs—could help U.S. agriculture make some difficult adjustments that ultimately could be forced upon the sector by economic forces.

I foresee the prospect for conservation-driven policy to contribute substantially to the resolution of at least some of agriculture's most pressing economic weaknesses. The policies are already proven winners in terms of erosion control. If others come to share this view and see this added potential, we just might deliver on those very big promises made for the conservation title of the 1985 farm bill.

Comments by Senator Sam Nunn
on the introduction of S.2937
in the second session of the 99th Congress

By Mr. Nunn (for himself and Mr. Cochran):

S. 2937. A bill to amend the Food Security Act of 1985 to increase the number of acres placed in the conservation reserve program, and for other purposes: to the Committee on Agriculture, Nutrition, and Forestry.

Increase in number of acres in the conservation reserve program.

Mr. Nunn. Mr. President, despite record government expenditures made to farmers through our commodity programs, the economic crisis in agriculture persists, and may even grow more serious. The 100th Congress will face early in 1987 some very tough budgetary decisions, including the possible need to save the Farm Credit System through a multi-billion-dollar infusion of funds. Regrettably, to address these critical problems, it now appears to me that Congress must reconsider decisions made just a year ago upon passage of the 1985 farm bill.

The programs authorized by that bill have already proven far too costly and ineffective. Moreover, costs will go up even higher next year without action by Congress. Commodity program expenditures also threaten to set back other vital missions of the Department of Agriculture which would, in the long run, contribute far more to the prosperity and sustainability of U.S. agriculture. We are falling short in export promotion efforts, in research and education, in our grain inspection and other quality assurance programs, and in conservation.

This legislation I introduce today on behalf of myself and Senator Cochran would accelerate accomplishment of one long overdue adjustment in our agriculture policy, an adjustment authorized and set in motion in the historic conservation title of the 1985 farm bill. It will both help in our our ongoing efforts to control erosion, and contribute to pressing near-term production adjustment and income support efforts.

We introduce this bill today because we are convinced that the conservation reserve program (CRP) authorized by subtitle D of section XII in the Food Security Act of 1985 can play an increasingly vital role in controlling soil erosion, protecting water quality, and supporting farm income. Indeed, the tremendous success of the program to date has led us to propose this legislation. We have three major goals in mind in offering this legislation.

First, accelerating enrollment into the CRP in 1987, with a goal of enrolling at least 35 million additional acres in the reserve;

Second, authorizing expansion of the reserve to 65 million acres, assuming the need exists to draw out of cultivation additional highly erodible cropland; and

Third, mandating the Secretary of Agriculture to begin, at least on a pilot program basis, the use of the reserve in addressing serious regional water quality or supply problems. Critical ground water quality problems in northwestern Iowa, and parts of Nebraska with sandy soils, are prime candidates for pilot projects.

We recognize that passage of this legislation is not possible in the 99th Congress. We are introducing the bill now, however, to alert our colleagues on the Committee of Agriculture, Nutrition, and Forestry and other Senators of our conviction that expansion of the conservation reserve should be vigorously pursued. We are also anxious to hear from the Department of Agriculture regarding this legislation, and encourage the executive branch to advise the Congress as soon as possible about its plans and intentions to expand CRP enrollment in early 1987, while also pursuing the other goals of this legislation.

My hope is that this legislation will help alert the agricultural community to a major opportunity that I believe now exists. Clearly, farmers across the Nation will benefit from strong steps to further reduce acreage planted to surplus crops, particularly in feedgrain producing regions. For this reason, and because the rate of signup has been disappointing in the Midwest, the legislation provides the Secretary with a clear mandate, and new authority to provide prospective CRP enrollees with adequate incentives to assure that the target level of enrollment is reached. This authority includes the following:

First, for producers with Farmers Home Administration financing, debt restructuring plans may include special provisions for advance CRP payments in cash or kind.

Second, the Secretary may offer a base acreage retirement bonus payment in cash or kind, to producers willing to surrender upon signup into the CRP commodity program base acres proportional to the acreage enrolled in the CRP.

Third, the Secretary may offer up to 50 percent of total 10-year CRP payments upon signup, in cash or kind, subject to a suitable mechanism to assure that the provisions of the CRP contract will be enforced.

Fourth, the Secretary may, on a State-by-State basis, authorize the use of CRP lands for grass, hay, and pasture uses, if the Secretary determines that such uses will not have an adverse affect on established operations in the State currently producing livestock, hay, or grass based silage.

We offer this legislation now to give the many individuals or organizations vitally interested in the conservation reserve time to fully study and reflect upon the best ways to achieve the legislation's basic intent, before major farm program changes are debated in early 1987. The shared sense of commitment expressed by a board diversity of groups and agricultural leaders toward the basic goals of the CRP has deeply impressed us, and has been a very positive force in bringing this new program into place. Let's build on this common ground, and follow the sound principles of the CRP in addressing additional problems related to water use and other environmental problems associated with agricultural production. By moving ahead with new ideas, we feel confident that the conservation reserve will meet the very high expectations of the Congress and the agricultural community.

S.2937
To amend the Food Security Act of 1985 to increase the number of acres planted in the conservation reserve program, and for other purposes.
In the Senate of the United States,
October 16 (legislative day, October 14), 1986.

Mr. Nunn (for himself and Mr. Cochran) introduced the following bill; which was read twice and referred to the Committee on Agriculture, Nutrition, and Forestry.

A Bill to amend the Food Security Act of 1985 to increase the number of acres placed in the conservation reserve program, and for other purposes.

Be it enacted by the Senate and House of Representatives of the United States of America in Congress assembled,

Section 1. Expansion of Conservation Reserve: (a) Acreage requirement—Section 1231 of the Food Security Act of 1985 (16 U.S.C. 3831) is amended—(1) by striking out subsection (b) and inserting in lieu thereof the following: "(b)(1) The Secretary shall enter into contracts with owners and operators of farms and ranches containing highly erodible cropland to place in the conservation reserve—"(A) during the 1986 crop year, not less than 5, nor more than 45, million acres; "(B) by December 31, 1987, not less than 45 million acres; and "(C) during the 1986 through 1990 crop years, not more than 65 million acres."; and (2) in subsection (c)(1)(B), by striking out "(5)" and inserting in lieu thereof "(1)(B)". (b) Inclusion of other lands.—Section 1231(c)(2) of such Act (16 U.S.C. 3831(c)(2)) is amended by adding at the end thereof the following new sentence: "Not later than August 1, 1987, the Secretary shall submit to the Committee on Agriculture of the House of Representatives and the Committee on Agriculture, Nutrition, and Forestry of the Senate a detailed plan and report indicating the manner in which the Secretary may implement this paragraph, including a discussion of the options for cooperating with agencies of State government in identifying areas to be subject to this paragraph and administering any program created under this paragraph.".

Sec. 2. Conservation Reserve Incentives. (a) Authority.—Section 1231(b) of the Food Security Act of 1985 (16 U.S.C. 3831(b)) (as amended by section 1(a)) is further amended by adding at the end thereof the following new paragraph: "(2) The Secretary may offer an owner or operator of land that is eligible to be placed in the conservation reserve such incentives as the Secretary determines are necessary to achieve the acreage requirements of paragraph (1)(B), including the incentives described in paragraphs (1) through (3) of section 1233(b).". (b) Incentives—(1) In general—Section 1233 of such Act (16 U.S.C. 3833) is amended—(A) by changing the title to read as follows: "Duties and powers of the Secretary"; (B) by inserting "(a)" after the section designation; and (C) by adding at the end thereof the following new subsection: "(b) To encourage an owner or operator to enter into a contract under this subtitle, the Secretary may—"(1) make an advance payment in cash or in-kind of up to 50 percent of the total amount of rental payments required to be paid under subsection (a)(2); "(2) make (in addition to any other payment authorized under this subtitle) a bonus payment in cash or in-kind to an owner or operator who retires permanently, from the cropland base and allotment history applicable to acreage placed in the reserve, a number of acres equal to the number of acres placed in the reserve; and "(3) permit a specified number of acres placed in the conservation reserve to be considered as reduced or set-aside acreage under an acreage limitatation or set-aside program established under section 107D(f), 105C(f), 103A(f), or 101A(f) of the Agricultural Act of 1949 (7 U.S.C. 1445b-3(f), 1444e(f), 1444-1(f), or 1441-1(f), if the Secretary determines that payments made under subsection (a)(2) are, on average, substantially less than payments made as a result of compliance with such program.''.

(2)Payment schedule—Section 1234(a)(2) of such Act (16 U.S.C. 3834(a)(2)) is amended—(A) by striking out ''or'' at the end of subparagraph (A); (B) by striking out the period at the end of subparagraph (B) and inserting in lieu thereof ''; or''; and (C) by adding at the end thereof the following new subparagraph: ''(C) as provided in section 1233(b)(1).''.

Sec. 3. Commerical use of conservation reserve acreage. Section 1232(a)(7) of the Food Security Act of 1985 (16 U.S.C. 3832 (a)(7)) is amended by striking out ''contract in response to a drought or other similar emergency'' and inserting in lieu thereof ''contract—''(A) in response to a drought or other similar emergency; or—''(B) if the Secretary ''(i) determines that allowing such commercial use would not have an adverse effect on existing commercial operations involving forage in the agricultural economy of the particular area in which the land is located; and ''(ii) makes a downward adjustment in the rental payments made or to be made under section 1233(a)(2) to reflect the probable economic return to the farm operation associated with the production of a forage crop on lands placed in the reserve.''.

Sec. 4. Ground water pilot program. Subtitle D of title XII of the Food Security Act of 1985 is amended by adding after section 1236 (16 U.S.C. 3836) the following new section: ''Ground water pilot program. ''Sec. 1237. (a) Not later than December 31, 1987, the Secretary shall formulate and carry out, through the 1990 crop year, a ground water pilot program, in conjuction with the conservation reserve program established under this subtitle, through contracts to assist owners and operators of land described in subsection (b) in conserving and improving the soil and water resources of their farms or ranches. ''(b)(1) Land is eligible to be placed in the pilot program established by this section if the land—''(A) is irrigated for the production of wheat, feed grains, or cotton in an area identified by an agency of the State or Federal government as subject to the overdraft of ground water; or ''(B) is associated with an aquifer adversely affected by such irrigation. ''(2) Eligible land shall also include cropland in that the Secretary determines, in consultation with State agricultural and resource use agencies, to be associated with water quality problems resulting from the irrigation described in paragraph (1), such as the contamination of underground aquifers by fertilizers or pesticides. ''(c) Under the terms of a contract entered into under this section, an owner or operator, in addition to fulfilling the obligations described in section 1232, must agree— ''(1) to retire permanently, from the base and allotment history applicable to acreage placed in the reserve, a number of acres equal to the number of acres placed in the reserve; and ''(2) not to use, for agricultural purposes, other land drawing from the same water supply as land placed in the reserve. ''(d)(1) Except where determined inappropriate by the Secretary, the Secretary shall contract with owners or operators of land described in subsection (b) in accordance with the terms and conditions provided in this subtitle. ''(2) The term 'highly erodible land' as used in this subtitle shall be considered to include land described in this section.''.

Sec. 5. Softwood timber. Section 608 of the Agricultural Program Adjustment Act of 1984 (7 U.S.C. 1981 note) is amended—(1) in subsection (a)(1)—(A) by striking out ''may'' the first place it appears and inserting in lieu thereof ''shall'', and (B) by striking out ''marginal land (as determined by the Secretary)'' and inserting in lieu thereof ''land''; and (3) in subsection (g), by striking out ''50,000'' and inserting in lieu thereof ''200,000''.

7

Matching conservation targets and instruments

Sandra S. Batie

Matching conservation targets and instruments is not an intellectually difficult task in the abstract. Challenges arise because conservation is only one of several competing agricultural policy goals; tradeoffs are inevitable. Because achieving some of one goal may necessarily mean less of another, the question of "How well are we doing?" can dissolve into "Which direction is forward?" In the case of the Food Security Act of 1985, the farm bill, the later question is particularly pertinent.

New targets for an old bill?

The farm bill was, for the most part, a continuation of existing programs. The surprise in the 1985 farm bill was the innovative nature of the conservation title in the legislation; the legislation included sodbuster, swampbuster, the conservation reserve, and conservation compliance provisions. The nature of the title exceeded the wildest dreams of conservationists (19). As one U.S. Department of Agriculture observer emphatically noted: "If someone would have told me at the beginning of 1985 that by the end of the year we would have conservation compliance, and the swampbuster in the law, or even have had a serious discussion of them, I would have thought they were...crazy..." (10).

There are at least two views why the conservation title remained intact and became law. The one view is that the farm bill of 1985, including the conservation title, was a classic case of incremental politics. The other perspective suggests a fundamental reorientation of agricultural policy.

The conservation title as incremental politics. Generally, political decisions make only incremental changes from the status quo; they rely on trial, error, and feedback. In some sense political solutions move away from problems more than they move toward objectives. This means that rarely do political decisions reflect action based on a perception of the right thing to do. Rather, political decisions arise from a process where conflicting values and interests of different partisan groups are accommodated as each group adjusts to objectives to earn some, but not complete, benefits for itself (*15*).

Clifford Hardin makes this observation with reference to the legislative horse-trading that goes on in the incremental politics of agricultural programs: "As a result legislators may sometimes pass measures which are not even favored by a Congressional majority. The bills pass, nevertheless, because that is how the modern Congress works" (*7*).

Most of the farm bill involved incremental changes from past bills. The argument that the 1985 conservation title was also incremental stems from the supportive nature of the conservation initiatives to a farm bill goal of limiting budget exposure through supply control. By removing some farmers from program benefits and some cropland from production, the conservation initiatives received support that had little to do with the environmental objectives.

This argument is consistent with history. From the late 1930s to the early 1970s, there was not great disparity between society's goals and actions with respect to agriculture's use of soil and water. As I argued elsewhere (*3*), much of the societal support for conservation during those years was support for stable agricultural income and for agricultural expansion. A broadly accepted argument was for public sector involvement in the private market economy to manage the nation's resource base, in part to promote the development of agriculture. The intent was to extend the nation's agrarian base and tradition through federal programs.

Soil and water conservation programs became a part of this social and political environment. There was public support for federally subsidized inputs, such as irrigation water; for production enhancing practices, such as soil fertilization and liming; and for agricultural expansion activities, such as drainage of wetlands. Soil conservation programs remained popular because they lowered farmers' operating costs, improved yields, and provided compensation for idling lands from production. The programs were not designed to achieve the most erosion control per program dollar spent. Selection criteria for the receipt of cost-sharing funds were not (until very recently) tied to the severity of a farmer's conservation problem, and conservation program benefits were spread widely. Soil conservation programs were not scrutinized for their effect on the soil resouce, nor was there a demand for scientific evaluations of their impact.

Conservation initiatives as part of the farm bills were supply control measures for the purposes of limiting budget exposure while supporting farm income. One view, then, is that the 1985 farm bill continues this tradition.

The conservation title as a reorientation of agricultural policy. An opposing view is that the conservation title represents the addition of a new target to the farm bill: environmental conservation. The view that conservation goals truly mattered in the 1985 farm bill implies that not all legislation can be explained as incremental partisan politics. Nonincremental changes are possible because it is the perception of broad social goals or ideologies that define the appropriateness of problem definitions and acceptable solutions. Congress is faced with many choices that allow ideology to be the decisive factor (*15*). The dominant ideology changes over time, and these shifts lead to institutional changes over time that alter the legitimate scope of government activity and provide for new operating rules that constrain subsequent periods of incremental politics (*15*).

Thus, one view of the reasons for passage of the conservation title is that farm legislation is in a transitional period where dominant ideologies are changing. The ideological change associated with environmental quality presents an opportunity for nonincremental shifts and new institutions to accommodate the new ideology. Proponents of the perspective that the conservation title was a major reorientation can demonstrate the influence of a new set of actors in the farm bill process. For the first time there was an active environmental coalition demonstrating that there was public support for the new program targets.

The environmental movement of the 1970s brought into question the ideology of the New Deal farm programs. For example, the traditional New Deal viewpoint saw people (often the farmer) as a manager of nature extracting a bounty to support the continued material prosperity of the nation. To environmentalists, peoples' manipulation of nature for solely material gain was unethical. The blending of this ethical argument with the argument that human survival depends upon a harmonious relation with the natural world has had widespread impact on public thought (*3*).

The expansion of agriculture in the 1970s and a recognition of its changing structure provided an impetus for environmentalists to investigate agriculture's relationship with the environment. The new image of the farmer as corporate businessperson weakened the historical rationale for the continued existence of natural resource programs to support agriculture and subjected farmers' use of resources to more careful public review and regulation. Agriculture began to lose its claim to special societal support (*3*).

During the 1985 farm bill debate, the environmental community made the argument that farm program expenditures were not in harmony with many societal values. Furthermore, for the first time data was available to demonstrate that the conservation initiatives could have an impact on environmental quality and could be enforceable.

Matching conservation targets and instruments

The two perspectives can both be right. While there are inescapable problems of choice and tradeoff with three farm bill goals—farm income support, limiting budget exposure, and improved soil and water quality—the objectives (or targets) reinforced one another to the extent that supporters of each objective were willing to help each other pass the bill. The bundling of the pursuit of several objectives into a few policy instruments for political acceptability comes at a cost. Unless each policy target has a separate instrument, the various targets may all be ill-served. Consider the two major conservation instruments—the conservation reserve and conservation compliance provisions of the 1985 farm bill.

The conservation reserve. Farm income support is a main target of the bill, and the instruments for achieving it are the loan program and deficiency payments. Supply control is a vehicle for limiting budget exposure. The main instrument for supply control is the acreage reduction program, wherein eligibility for loan and deficiency payments is conditioned on reductions in acreage planted to program crops. This is accomplished in the farm bill by acreage limitations, set-asides, and required diversions.

Whether the CRP can double as a supply control program will be a function of several variables. These are the participation rates of farmers, the number of acres placed in the CRP, the erosion control potential of the CRP, the protection of nonreserved acres, the production on nonreserved acres, and the management of nonreserved acres.

While historically the use of conservation reserves to obtain both soil erosion control and supply control has had limited success (*1*), the 1985 CRP has the opportunity to improve the instruments by which supply control and conservation targets are to be obtained. This was partly addressed in the language of the 1985 farm bill. The CRP is to be targeted to the most fragile or highly erodible croplands. This is now defined as those lands currently cropped in Soil Conservation Service land capability classes VI-VIII or class II-V lands now cropped that are eroding at more than three times the SCS-determined tolerance rate (3T or greater). There are an estimated 60 million to 70 million acres of such land nationwide, 45 million acres of which are mandated by legislation to be retired over a five-year period (16). In exchange for an annual payment, landowners agree not to produce on this cropland for 10 years.

For the CRP to provide supply control, it must include croplands that would otherwise have been placed in commodity crops. However, as the CRP is presently designed, if the participating farm has a commodity program base, the total base will be reduced because of participation in the CRP. Taft and Runge (16) refer to this as the "base bite." As a result, the more farmer benefits associated with participation, the more a farmer will require in payment.

The higher the farm program benefits, the more valuable are acres for the ARP aspects of the commodity programs. The ARP idles these acres for only one year at a time; there is an incentive to establish as large a historical cropping use as possible to obtain a higher base. Thus, there are fewer acres for the CRP.

As Taft and Runge summarized: "The ironic and troubling result of these program interactions is the ARPs fail to control supply due to slippage, which in turn causes the CRP to lose eligible acres due to the crowding out effect. In addition, the base bite effect raises the opportunity cost of CRP participation and, thus, CRP bids. These conflicts frustrate both supply control and conservation objectives at the same time that they make both programs less cost-effective. The evidence from the first two rounds of CRP bidding supports this argument" (16).

Historic response to this type of conflict is to emphasize one goal: farm income. That is, conservation goals were essentially ignored, the slippage in obtaining supply control was allowed to continue, and international market implications were ignored. In the long-standing tradition of most targeted federal programs—be they urban renewal or commodity supply control—they become untargeted, widely distributed programs (9).

Conservation compliance. The conservation compliance provision of the farm bill makes all persons already cultivating highly erodible cropland ineligible for price support loans, purchases, and payments for program crops; for lands insured or guaranteed by the Farmers Home Administration; for federal crop insurance; and for disaster payments unless they obtain a conservation plan by 1990 for the eroding cropland and implement that plan by 1995.

If conservation compliance and the CRP were fully implemented so that every eligible acre as identified by the current erodibility (EI) standard[1] had erosion rates of 2T or below, soil erosion would be reduced by 1.2 billion tons annually—46 percent of all erosion on cropland (18). Of this, perhaps 400 million tons of sediment per year would be prevented from entering surface waters (11). Six hundred million tons of soil or 20 percent of all soil loss from cropland will be conserved because of the conservation compliance program, according to Gary Margheim with the Soil Conservation Service.

However, the extent to which conservation compliance achieves these levels of soil conservation or the impacts on supply control will depend on many factors. These include the eligibility standards, compliance standards, enforcement, and future farm program participation.

For example, the current eligibility standard for highly eroding land is an EI equal to or greater than 8. Approximately 118 million acres of cropland are considered highly erodible by this standard. This is 28 percent of the nation's cropland; it accounts for 58 percent of all of the cropland erosion in excess of 1T (18).

There is not, however, a one-to-one correspondence in the use of the EI as the standard and the use of soil tolerance limits. Of the 118 million acres identified with an EI equal to or greater than 8, for example, almost half (47 percent), or 54 million acres, is being farmed in a way to reduce erosion below 2T (5). At the same time, the EI-equal-to-or-greater-than-8 standard exempts land that has excessive rates of erosion despite a low physical potential. There are an estimated 40 million acres that are eroding above 2T but are not accommodated within the EI-equal-to-or-greater-than-8 definition (5).

Thus, different eligibility standards—different EIs, or use of soil tolerance limits—result in different acres being affected. The potential and direct impact on the environment and commodity supply will depend in part on the choice of the definition of what is to be considered highly eroding lands.

No matter how stringently the regulations are designed and enforced, conservation compliance will have an impact only to the extent that the

---

[1]EI is defined as the maximum predicted average annual rate of erosion divided by the average soil loss tolerance, or T. EI thus can be interpreted as the multiple the land would erode over T without a cover crop or conserving practices. Higher values of EI imply higher erosion potential.

lands designated as highly erodible are controlled by participants in the various farm programs. Currently, farm programs have high enrollments. The 1986 commodity programs attracted 85 percent of the corn acreage, 84 percent of the wheat acreage, and 91 percent of the upland cotton acreage (*18*). Studies conducted prior to these high enrollments concluded that conservation compliance would not attract large numbers of fragile landowners if they had to comply with low erosion control requirements (*2, 12, 13*).

Reichelderfer (*14*) examined eight areas of the country that had critical erosion problems. She concluded that, in a given year, between one-half and three-fourths of the cropland eroding above five tons per acre per year is operated by individuals not participating in commodity or USDA conservation-cost sharing programs. She stated, "Efforts to increase the consistency of USDA commodity and conservation programs would contribute little to overcoming the nation's total erosion problems" (*14*). Clark (*4*) concluded that conservation compliance offers more potential to eliminate program inconsistencies than to achieve soil conservation.

It is difficult to estimate the ultimate impact on farm income (or budget outlays) of the compliance programs until there is an estimate of how many farmers will exit the program rather than comply, how many of the program participants actually control the highly erodible lands, and how nonparticipants will adjust their cropping patterns. For example, if many farmers exit [remain in] the programs and increase [decrease] their planted acreage, market prices could decline [increase] because of the program's existence.

For those farmers who participate, however, it is not necessarily true that highly erodible lands are also those that are marginal and nonproductive (*13*). Studies of set-aside programs, for example, show that the distribution of diverted acres by land capability class tend to reflect the same distribution as cultivated cropland (*17*). This may mean that lands removed from commodity crops either for compliance or to be part of the conservation reserve may be more productive than the acres farmers have elected to divert from production in the past.

If these lands are diverted and if slippage—increased production on nondiverted acres—is not too great, then supply of commodities may indeed decline. However, if many farmers choose not to comply and exit the programs and the program acreage reduction obligations no longer apply, then the commodity crop supply could increase, market prices could weaken, and farm program costs ultimately could rise.

Conservation compliance as defined in the 1985 farm bill fulfills several of the motivations that accounted for its initial support. It removes many of the apparent program inconsistencies, and it provides a strong ethical statement that social obligations attend farm program benefits. It is less clear how much actual environmental improvement will result from the implementation of the conservation compliance program, regardless of how stringently the regulations are designed, due to the uncertainities associated with farm program participation. Thus, conservation compliance cannot be considered a carefully crafted instrument for attainment of any of the farm bill targets.

The farm bill of 1987

Today, the farm bill is the subject of congressional concern only a year after its passage, in part, because it does not reflect any dominant ideology. "The agricultural programs are a philosophical jungle containing elements of free-market risk and federal bail outs, capitalist entrepreneurship and socialist central planning.... [They] do not reinforce anyone's world view" (6). It is also becoming more widely known that most farm program benefits go to the least financially stressed farmers. A U.S. General Accounting Office study found that 63 percent of farm program benefits went to farmers with a debt-to-asset ratio of less than 40 percent. Sensational newspaper stories of farms receiving millions of dollars in program benefits, despite a $50,000 payment limitation, undermine support of the farm bill as a vehicle for improving farm income. Moreover, as the U.S. agricultural economy is increasingly integrated into the world economy, the farm bill, as it currently is structured with loan programs, deficiency payments, and supply control, is seen as self-defeating. Many argue it takes a natural comparative advantage in agriculture and turns it into a competitive disadvantage with tremendous surpluses and incompetitive prices. Finally, the farm bill is seen as causing damage to environmental quality by encouraging and supporting unnecessarily large acreages for growing crops that are associated with heavy chemical use and with soil erosion.

To what degree does the farm bill structure incentives to participants so as to reflect accurately society's informed judgment about appropriate resource allocations—to wealthy and to poorer farmers, to the international community, to the federal budget, and to environmental quality? The answer in any dimension appears to be "not very well."

One possibility is to pursue improvements through incremental adjustments to the current farm bill. One proposal is to improve the bill by designating separate instruments to achieve separate objectives. For example, use the ARP for supply control and the CRP for environmental quality. Taft and Runge (16) develop this idea carefully. They propose that land be divided by soil types ranked on the basis on their productivity and their resistance to erosion. Lands that are both resistant to erosion and productive should be used for production—thus ensuring the least-cost production of our crops. Lands that are resistant to erosion but not productive should not receive any program benefits. Lands that are not resistant to erosion but are highly productive should be in short-term acreage reduction programs, and lands that are not productive and not resistant to erosion should be in the CRP.

Where supply control and maintenance of the soil resource are the chief objectives, the logic of the Taft and Runge framework is compelling. This distinction leaves the farmer producing on lower-cost acres and, therefore, maintains the competitive position. With more research, the Taft-Runge proposal could be altered to better encompass water quality concerns as well.

It may also be an excellent time for intellectual entrepreneurs to concentrate their energies on the targets of social policy and lay the groundwork for some nonincremental changes in policy. For example, public support for farm income is not unconditional. Maintenance of a system that provides assistance for the more needy farmers without sacrificing international comparative advantages appears to be a viable target that the public is willing to afford. Thus, the policies that have defendable criteria for assisting these farmers have merit. Proposals for defensible and politically viable means of achieving income (but not price support) for sections of the farming community—the so called uncoupling of farm policy—is achieving increased visibility. This would mean that farmers would produce what the market prices indicated were potentially profitable and not generate the huge surpluses of commodity program crops. It is probable that such a result would mean fewer agricultural chemicals as well as less fragile cropland in use.

For another example, one target is the protection and improvement of water quality. Policies can be designed that obtain the production rights on certain lands that contribute to surface water and groundwater pollution problems, perhaps by the purchase of conservation easements. Indeed, it is possible to interpret the language of implementation of a reserve based on water quality protection criteria. The focus would be not on supply control but on water quality benefits.

Each of these ideas for policy change has drawbacks and also suffers from the lack of careful analysis of the impacts of their implementation on such important factors as farm and nonfarm employment, farm structure, rural economies, consumer prices, and environmental quality. Nevertheless, there is need for increased attention to the values the public associates with the farm bill (targets) and to public expenditures (instruments) more appropriately allocated to reflect the values. It is time for reflection on "which direction is forward," and there remains an obligation to pursue that direction whenever possible.

REFERENCES

1. Batie, Sandra S. 1984. *Agricultural policy and soil conservation implications for the 1985 Farm Bill.* American Enterprise Institute Occasional Papers. American Enterprise Institute, Washington, D.C.
2. Batie, Sandra S., and A. G. Sappington. 1985. *Cross-compliance as a soil conservation strategy: A case study.* In Sandra S. Batie and David E. Ervin [editors] *Farm Level Impacts of Adopting Cross-Compliance Programs: Policy Implications.* Department of Agricultural Economics, University of Missouri, Columbia. pp. 44-64.
3. Batie, Sandra S., Leonard A. Shabman, and Randall A. Kramer. 1986. *U.S. agricultural and natural resource policy: Past and future.* In C. Ford Runge [editor] *The Future of the North American Granary: Politics, Economics and Resource Constraints in North American Agriculture.* Iowa State Press, Ames.
4. Clark, Richard T. 1984. *Cross-compliance between USDA price and income support programs and soil conservation.* Economic Research Service, U.S. Department of Agriculture, Washington, D.C.
5. Dicks, Michael R., and Jim Vertrees. 1986. *Improving the payoff from the conservation reserve program.* In Daniel W. Halbach, C. Ford Runge, and William E. Larson [eds.] *Making Soil and Water Conservation Work: Scientific and Policy Perspectives.* Soil Conservation Society of America, Ankeny, Iowa. pp. 109-117.
6. Easterbrook, Gregg. 1985. *Making sense of agriculture.* The Atlantic Monthly (July): 63-78.
7. Hardin, Clifford M. 1986. *Congress is the problem.* Choices 1(1): 6-11.
8. House, Robert, C. W. Ogg, K. C. Clayton, and J. D. Johnson. 1981. *USDA incentives study.* Draft. Economics Research Service, U.S. Department of Agriculture, Washington, D.C.
9. John, Dewitt. 1987. *American federalism in a turbulent world economy.* Draft. National Governor's Association, Washington, D.C.
10. Leman, Christopher. 1987. *The uses of knowledge: Ideas, information and the political context in food and agricultural policymaking.* Draft. Resources for the Future, Washington, D.C.
11. Margheim, Gary. 1986. *Implementing conservation compliance provisions of the Food Security Act of 1985.* In Proceedings, 1986 Outlook Conference. U.S. Department of Agriculture, Washington, D.C.
12. Ogg, Clayton W. 1985. *Cross-compliance proposals and fragile croplands.* In Sandra S. Batie and David E. Ervin [editors] *Farm Level Impacts of Adopting Cross-Compliance Programs: Policy Implications.* Department of Agricultural Economics, University of Missouri, Columbia. pp. 9-25.
13. Ogg, C. W., Shwu-eng Webb, and Wen-Yuan Huang. 1984. *Cropland acreage reduction alternatives: An economic analysis of a soil conservation reserve and competitive bids.* Journal of Soil and Water Conservation 39(6): 379-383.
14. Reichelderfer, Katherine H. 1985. *Do USDA farm program participants contribute to soil erosion?* Economic Research Service, U.S. Department of Agriculture, Washington, D.C.

15. Shabman, Leonard A. 1984. *Water resources management: Policy economics for an era of transitions.* Southern Journal of Agricultural Economics (July): 53-66.
16. Taft, Steven, and C. Ford Runge. 1986. *Supply control, conservation, and budget restraint: Conflicting instruments in the 1985 farm bill.* Staff Paper P86-33. Department of Agricultural and Applied Economics, University of Minnesota, St. Paul.
17. U.S. Department of Agriculture. 1984. *Conservation benefits of 1983 PIK and acreage reduction programs, a preliminary report.* Washington, D.C.
18. U.S. Department of Agriculture. 1986. *U.S. Department of Agriculture environmental assessment for the highly erodible land conservaton provisions of the Food Security Act of 1985.* Washington, D.C.
19. Ward, Justin. 1986. *The Conservation reserve and the rural environment.* Environment 28(7): 3-5.

8

Improving the payoff from the Conservation Reserve Program

Michael R. Dicks and Jim Vertrees

In the 1980s there has been substantial progress in bringing public policy to bear on "highly erodible cropland." Public concern about environmental damages from soil erosion and excess productive capacity combined to spawn new federal conservation programs in the 1985 Food Security Act. One such program, the Conservation Reserve Program, is designed to remove highly erodible cropland from the cropland base while reducing taxpayer costs of supporting the prices of surplus crops. Thus far the CRP has proven somewhat successful. But its performance can be improved upon if scarce public resources are more appropriately targeted to well-defined objectives.

In theory, government programs, including those oriented toward conservation, should be targeted to maximize social welfare. For long-term land retirement programs, specific cropland should be targeted to maximize the reduction in on-site and off-site environmental damages and the increase in recreational value and supply-control cost savings. The order in which these benefits are maximized should be determined by society's preferences.

The current program

For the first time since 1956 major soil conservation provisions are included in a farm bill. Chief among these provisions are the CRP, conservation compliance, and sodbuster provisions. Because the CRP was the first provision to be implemented and promises a significant reduction in soil erosion, it is currently the centerpiece of new conservation policy.

CRP objectives. The objectives of the CRP are to (1) reduce wind and water erosion, (2) protect the nation's long-term capability to produce food and fiber, (3) reduce sedimentation, (4) improve water quality, (5) create better habitat for fish and wildlife, (6) curb production of surplus commodities, and (7) provide needed income support for farmers.

CRP implementation. Owners or operators with "highly erodible" cropland may submit bids to the U.S. Department of Agriculture to retire that land from crop production for 10 years, receiving in return annual rental payments and half the cost of establishing permanent cover. For initial bidding periods in March, May, and August 1986, eligibility was limited to 69.5 million acres in land capability classes II-V eroding at greater than three times the tolerance level(T) and all cropland in land capability classes VI-VIII (to be referred to as 3T). Rental rate caps were established for state and substate areas (pools) based on prevailing land values and cash rents for each area. All bids at or below pool caps on rental rates were accepted.

CRP performance. Total enrolled acreage for the CRP reached 8.9 million acres through the August sign-up. The sign-up was heaviest in the Mountain and Southern Plains regions, and lighest in the Northeast, Appalchia, and Corn Belt (Table 1). The average government cost of placing these 8.9 million acres into permanent cover was approximately $97 per acre, consisting of about $47 per acre for annual rental payments and an initial $50 for cover establishment costs. The total annual expenditure for the first year of sign-ups was about $865 million. The benefits of this expenditure include long-run productivity gains from reductions in annual soil erosion by some 215 million tons, a reduction in off-site damages caused by the erosion, and direct and indirect supply-control cost savings equal to somewhere between 70 percent and 85 percent of first-year expenditures for the CRP.

Targeting to achieve objectives

The ultimate performance of the CRP depends upon the combination of objectives actually pursued and the criteria used to achieve these objectives. Specific objectives can be targeted for emphasis through choice of (1) eligibility requirements, (2) bid pool sizes, and (3) bid selection criteria. These criteria can be used to focus the program on specific cropland acres, with a specified distribution among regions, states, and counties yielding specific social benefits upon retirement. Thus, targeting should begin with the basic questions not only of what is being targeted but also, more importantly, of what objective can be achieved using this target.

The reduction of erosion by removing from the productive base as much erodible land as possible is often viewed as an end in itself. However, erosion reduction in some areas may provide important benefits to the land owner or operator but only limited benefits to society. Erosion reduction in other areas may provide limited private benefits but large social benefits. In the latter case, rather than reducing erosion per se, a more efficient approach might be to maximize the benefits generated per ton of erosion reduced.

So far, implementation of the CRP has emphasized the removal of as much erodible land as possible. For the first three bidding rounds in 1986, this targeting was achieved through the eligibility criteria. That is, only 69.5 million acres of the total 420 million acres of cropland were considered "highly erodible" and therefore eligible for bidding. Acreage allotments for state or substate pools were not implemented, allowing most of the enrollment to occur in certain areas. The bid selection procedures

Table 1. Preliminary summary of the March, May, and August signups for the Conservation Reserve Program, October 1, 1986.

Region	Total Cropland	Eligible Acres	Acres Accepted	Percent Eligible Acres Accepted	Bids	Acres /Bid	Average Rental Rate ($/acre)	Rental Rate ($/acre)
	----------1,000 acres----------							
Northeast	17,268	2,336	41.3	1.8	1,174	35.2	54.96	50-65
Appalachian	22,555	4,973	313.3	6.3	6,603	47.4	52.13	45-60
Southeast	18,324	2,438	490.9	20.1	7,418	66.2	38.94	40-60
Delta States	21,909	1,734	278.3	16.0	3,826	72.7	40.61	40-50
Corn Belt	92,421	16,171	885.7	5.5	13,101	67.6	65.91	40-90
Lake States	43,961	4,414	774.0	17.5	9,999	77.4	53.67	20-85
Northern Plains	93,633	9,377	1,369.1	14.6	11,202	122.2	46.16	28-70
Southern Plains	44,819	12,925	1,578.6	12.2	6,837	230.9	39.48	35-55
Mountain	43,219	11,840	2,445.3	20.7	6,579	371.7	38.92	33-50
Pacific	22,683	3,226	749.1	23.2	2,115	354.2	48.67	50-65
US Total	420,792	69,436	8,925.6	12.9	68,854	129.6	45.50	20-90

Source: *Agricultural Outlook*, October 1986, ERS, USDA.

relied entirely on rental payment caps, above which bids were not selected. However, selection of qualifying bids did implicitly consider reduction of surplus crop production and minimization of government expenditures, as well as erosion reduction.

Defining eligible cropland as land with erosion greater than three times the soil loss tolerance level (T) indirectly emphasized the reduction in on-site damages from excessive erosion. The rental rate caps reflect the average productivity within state or substate pools and enable higher bids to be accepted in pools with more productive lands. However, within pools, setting caps on the basis of average productivity tends to discriminate against more productive lands. Also, the rental caps create maximum limits on government expenditures for the CRP. In brief, the current CRP is directed toward removing as much erodible cropland as possible from production, with some weight given to government cost and little weight, if any, given to the benefits generated from a reduction in off-site damages.

Alternative targeting schemes

Eligibility requirements, bid pool size, and bid selection criteria could be used to place the highest priority on one or more specific CRP objectives.

Eligibility. Employment of a restrictive definition of "highly erodible" would limit the number of acres eligible and favor erosion reduction over other objectives. Relaxing the definition would increase the number of eligible acres, allowing greater flexibility in targeting other objectives. The larger the eligible acreage, the greater the likelihood of receiving more bids to retire land having a wider range of characteristics. More bids of wider variety would simply increase the opportunity to achieve specific goals.

For example, if reducing environmental damage caused by soil erosion were the highest priority, a restrictive definition could eliminate from eligibility those lands whose retirement would yield the largest environmental benefits. Expanding eligibility from the current 3T definition to 2T would increase the number of eligible acres from 69.5 million to 104 million. Changing the eligibility to the erodibility index (potential erosion) criteria currently used for the Highly Erodible Land Conservation provisions (Subtitle C, Title XII, 1985 Food Security Act) would also increase the number of eligible acres. But almost 54 million acres (47 percent) of the 118 million acres of cropland meeting the Highly Erodible Land Conservation definition ($EI \geq 8$) are eroding at less than 2T. As a result, the actual acreage with excessive erosion ($\geq 2T$) is, under the $EI \geq 8$ criterion, reduced to about 63 million acres (Figure 1). Further, the EI ≥ 8 criterion would exclude 20 million acres of the approximately 70 million acres eroding in excess of 3T.

Bid pool size. Acreage allotments could be devised for regions, states, or substate pools to increase the potential benefits from erosion reduction, supply control, or income support. The CRP already has an implicit acreage allotment in the legislation's requirement that every effort be made to put 5 million acres into commercial timber. This encourages enrollment in the Southeast, which has a favorable tree-growing climate and markets for logs and pulp (95 percent of the timber plantings are in the southeastern states).

Bid selection criteria. Different objectives can also be emphasized by using alternative bid selection "formulas." Four such formulas are shown here using the March sign-up to illustrate their effort on the program's performance (Table 2). The formulas are defined as follows:

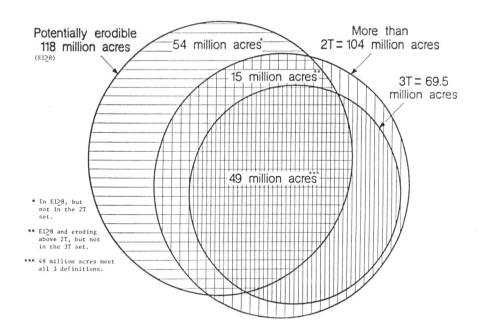

Potentially erodible 118 million acres (EI ≥ 8)

54 million acres*

More than 2T = 104 million acres

3T = 69.5 million acres

15 million acres**

49 million acres***

* In EI ≥ 8, but not in the 2T set.

** EI ≥ 8 and eroding above 2T, but not in the 3T set.

*** 49 million acres meet all 3 definitions.

Figure 1. Relationship between sets of cropland eligible for the conservation reserve program under alternative definitions of "highly erodible" land. Source: *Agricultural Outlook,* **October 1986, ERS, USDA.**

Rental: the current method based on maximum bid caps.

Erosion: maximizes the tons of erosion reduction per acre.

Supply: maximizes the per acre cost savings in supply control.

Combined: maximizes the per acre value of supply control and erosion reduction, assuming a one-to-one relationship between tons of erosion and environmental benefits.

All of the criteria were applied to the bids received, and selection was constrained to the actual level of expenditure for the March sign-up. The current criterion, minimizing *rental* cost, had the lowest per acre cost for rental payments, but showed the poorest overall performance in meeting CRP's multiple objectives. Targeting *erosion* markedly increased the per acre reduction in soil loss and, consequently, had the lowest cost per ton of erosion reduced. The maximum *supply* control formula reduced supply-control costs more than the current selection criteria without sacrificing the per acre reduction in soil erosion. The *combined* formula, targeting to supply control, cost savings, and erosion reduction, offered the greatest overall benefits.

The performances of the various criteria differ more dramatically as the number of bids to select from increases. Eligibility requirements, bid pool size, and bid selection criteria could be used to further increase the private

Table 2. Analysis of alternative bid selection criteria—summary of all March 1986 bids submitted.

	Rental*	Erosion†	Supply‡	Combined§
Acres accepted (1,000)	828	712	659	730
Rental costs per acre ($)	42	50	54	49
Erosion reduction per acre (ton)	26	47	25	41
Rental costs per ton of erosion ($)	1.61	1.07	2.16	1.2
Supply control savings per acre ($)	16	17	32	25

Source: Preliminary analysis prepared by Bill Boggess, ERS, USDA.
*Minimize rental costs—select bids on the basis of lowest rental cost per acre subject to $35 million expediture.
†Maximize erosion reduction—select bids on the basis of the lowest cost per ton of erosion subject to $35 million expenditure.
‡Maximize supply control—select bids on the basis of the lowest cost per dollar of supply control cost savings for a $35 million expenditure.
§Maximize erosion reduction and supply control—select bids on the basis of the net cost (rental rate-supply control cost savings) per ton of erosion subject to a $35 million expenditure.

and social benefits of the CRP if the value of reducing off-site damage could be incorporated into the formula.

Feasibility of targeting environmental objectives

If targeting is to focus on the benefits of reducing environmental (on-site and off-site) damages as well as supply control and government cost, then the current effort must be redirected. Unfortunately, redirecting the focus of the CRP in favor of reducing environmental damage will be difficult for several reasons. First, information about the relationship between soil erosion and environmental damage is sketchy at best, and implementation at the national level would be impractical. But it is possible for states to identify those situations where the use of land for crop production causes significant environmental damages. In fact, with some foresight the Congress added a provision in the CRP legislation that allows the secretary of agriculture to include any acreage that poses a "serious environmental threat," even if it is not highly erodible. Thus, states could help identify those acres and, if necessary, provide added incentives to farmers to remove that land from crop production. Granting eligibility based on "serious environmental threat" could allow for inclusion of land contributing to salinity and selenium loadings, groundwater depletion areas, buffer strips to intercept pollutants entering water bodies, and former wetlands. Their inclusion would add at least 25 million acres to the land already eligible for the CRP by virtue of its erodibility[1]. However, the differences between state estimates of the value of environmental damages could pose implementation problems. As of now, the CRP implicity assigns the same value to a unit reduction in wind and water erosion regardless of where the erosion occurs.

Second, targeting to reduce environmental damages could invite political problems of unequal distribution of public resources and benefits among regions, states, and congressional districts. For example, wind erosion is the predominant source of erosion in the West. The relationship between wind erosion and environmental damage is not well documented. Even if a good measure of the amount of soil leaving the field as a result of wind could easily be measured, the resulting damages would still be difficult to quantify. Thus, public funds are likely to be directed toward areas

[1] Ogg, Clayton, John E. Hostetler, and Donna J. Lee; "Environmental and Conservation Provisions for Broadening the Acreage Eligible for the Conservation Reserve," an unpublished paper, Economic Research Service, USDA.

where sheet and rill erosion constitute the prevalent problem because environmental damages from these types of erosion have better documentation.

Third, the nation is likely to remain in a prolonged period of budget austerity. This will severely limit the additional resources for new conservation programs at the national level. As a practical matter, selection criteria are likely to be weighted heavily in favor of supply-control cost savings.

Fourth, a targeting effort oriented toward off-site damages would require additional resources and involve higher adminstrative costs. Indeed, one of the clear benefits of using the erodibility index to determine eligibility would be a substantial savings in administrative costs. So it would be necessary, but difficult, to show that the benefits of reducing off-site damages exceed the higher costs of environmental targeting.

Finally, the methods and definitions used in implementing the three previous CRP sign-ups evolved from months of discussion and compromise among many professional organizations and government agencies. Any new procedures are likely to meet with resistance from several of these representatives.

Conclusion

Conservation goals have been linked to commodity programs under the 1985 Food Security Act, but improvements in the payoff from that linkage are possible. Ideally, programs should be targeted to achieve greater social benefits per dollar expended. States can play an important role, if not a leading role, in this process by helping to target the CRP to land whose retirement would yield social benefits.

Changes in the current program could be made to increase its cost effectiveness as opposed to the number of acres enrolled. In other words, whatever objectives for CRP are pursued, the social benefits and costs of attaining each objective should be identified and given desired weights. The weighted objectives can then be used in a formula to select bids so as to provide the greatest benefits per dollar expended without regard to the number of acres selected.

The effectiveness of using specific bid selection criteria to target cropland for retirement will depend largely on the number of bids submitted. The number of bids will depend upon eligibility requirements, competing programs, and the learning curve for eligible participants. Thus, participation should increase with less restrictive eligiblity requirements, less attractive commodity programs, and better dissemination of information on the CRP and the conservation compliance requirements.

III

State soil and water conservation policy

9

Linking state and federal policy: The RIM initiative

Greg Larson

In the early years of soil conservation, state and local governments had little incentive to develop soil and water conservation programs. The reason was obvious: Leadership, policy development, and land treatment were implemented by the federal government through soil and water conservation districts.

But in a trend that began in the 1970s and which is now accelerating, local and state governments are discovering that the federal government has greatly reduced the financing of soil conservation programs. Of necessity, therefore, many states have developed their own initiatives to complement reordered federal priorities and address unique state or local problems. Examples include administrative, managerial, and technical training programs for conservation district personnel, cost-sharing programs, soil loss controls, and agricultural land preservation efforts.

As federal fiscal policies mandate the decentralization of many programs, it is essential that states and local units of government be prepared to take advantage of every opportunity afforded to them. Minnesota, for example, has adopted an approach to integrating federal policy in an attempt to derive maximum benefits from soil conservation programs.

A coalition for action

Early in 1985, Minnesota lawmakers were joined by statewide environmental, sportsmen, and farm groups to create a state-funded resource protection and conservation reserve program popularly known as the

Reinvest in Minnesota Resources Act of 1986 (RIM). The measure passed the Minnesota Legislature with only six dissenting votes. The new state initiative was an outgrowth of a 1984 governor's study on ways to improve the state's billion-dollar tourism industry through improvement of wildlife habitat and protection of soil and water resources.

Environmentalists, sportsmen, and farmers who support RIM say that the timing may never have been better to unite their common interests to reduce soil erosion and sedimentation in rural areas through conservation incentives, such as RIM. They point to a recent governor's policy study that reported more than half of Minnesota's 93,000 farm operations may be forced out of existence within a decade. This is reflected in 1984 data showing that the state lost 5,000 farms in one year. At the same time, more than half the state's cropland is eroding at levels exceeding T (the tolerance level), and of that cropland 21 percent is eroding at more than 2T.

Even though RIM was never intended to bail out financially strapped farmers, the cropland retirement provisions of one of its components— the RIM Reserve—could make the difference between quitting and survival for some farmers. Moreover, it could have a profoundly positive effect on Minnesota's lagging outdoor recreation businesses.

The financial importance of Minnesota's tourism industry prompted Governor Rudy Perpich in 1984 to form a committee of government, business, private, and nonprofit organization leaders to find ways to improve the state's outdoor recreation industry. In its final report the Citizens Commission on Hunting and Fishing drew a parallel between a private industry's reinvestment of its own capital and Minnesota's tourism industry. The commission recommended a reinvestment of at least six percent of the $1 billion that tourism brings to Minnesota each year. To this end, a $600-million, 10-year program was proposed. Land and water conservation initiatives, such as cost-sharing and land retirement, were slated to receive $150 million.

RIM is the result of the commission's recommendation. A portion of the 1986 RIM bill provides $10 million to the Minnesota Department of Agriculture for the RIM Conservation Reserve; another $6 million will be used by the Minnesota Department of Natural Resources for wildlife development projects and aspen recycling. Significantly, the appropriation established for RIM is a dedicated fund. Chances of success for the RIM initiative are much improved, given the atmosphere created by the conservation provisions of the 1985 federal farm bill. In particular, the Conservation Reserve Program in that bill bodes well as a complementary measure.

Despite a number of well-founded critiques, the Conservation Reserve

Program has been well received in Minnesota so far. After three sign-ups, Minnesota ranked third, both in total acres enrolled (661,292) and in total dollars obligated ($34,642,251), behind Colorado and Texas. The acreage by itself is staggering when one considers that it exceeds the total extent of state wildlife management areas by 130,000 acres. Performance of CRP is a credit to many individuals in both the public and private sector. And the success of CRP provides an appropriate basis for discussion of the RIM Reserve, an initiative that demonstrates state links to federal policy and, in particular, the conservation provisions of the 1985 farm bill.

The conservation provisions of the 1985 farm bill were long awaited and much needed. States with soil conservation targeting efforts, cost-sharing programs, or soil loss controls will now receive policy support from the federal government as a result of coherent conservation policies, namely, sodbuster, swampbuster, and cross-compliance. These provisions complement initiatives under way in many states. In Minnesota, 1982 legislation mandated the development of a targeting procedure for state cost-sharing funds. Early in the process, problems were encountered similar to those cited by Batie (1): difficulty in developing criteria for selecting target areas and determining the equitable distribution of public assistance.

Criteria that accommodated the required mix of issues—soil erosion and water quality—were established following an extensive analysis of the state using National Resources Inventory data, Minnesota Pollution Control Agency feedlot surveys, and the State Planning Agency geographic data base. The latter includes soil maps generalized to 640 acres. A formula was developed reflecting conservation district variations in soil erosion and water quality problems and land treatment costs. Conservation districts allocate these once-prioritized dollars using a combination of variable cost-share rates and land capability classification. In this manner, funds are—in policymakers' logic—equitably distributed. For example, higher cost-share rates (75 percent) are provided for more severe problems ($>2T$) and reduced rates (50 percent) are offered for less severe problems ($>T\text{-}2T$). Moreover, lands in land capability classes V through VIII are denied cost-sharing assistance. This policy of emphasizing treatment of bonafide cropland and denying cost-sharing assistance for marginal croplands was an appropriate foundation for the RIM initiative.

Enrollment options

Through the RIM Reserve, landowners are paid to take their marginal cropland out of production. Although RIM Reserve is similar to and complements the federal CRP, there are several differences between the programs. While CRP provides 10-year contracts with annual payments to participating farmers, RIM Reserve provides for the acquisition of 10-year or permanent easements.

For a 10-year easement, RIM Reserve provides a single lump-sum payment, or at the landowner's option, up to four equal, consecutive annual payments to cover the 10-year period. One-time payments and easements were not originally intended. Annual payments and contracts were originally proposed, but when general revenue bonds were used to fund the RIM program, lump-sum payments and easements became a requirement. As it turns out, easements may provide yet another link to the 1985 farm bill. Title XIII of the farm bill authorizes the Farmers Home Administration to use conservation easements to restructure farm debt or liquidate land acquired through loan default. In Minnesota there are 44,530 acres in the latter category, including 27,648 acres of cropland. Although many details have yet to be resolved, a pilot program in Minnesota to develop FmHA easements is being planned. Experience gained from the RIM Reserve easement process may, therefore, be timely.

Average accepted bids from the most recent round of CRP bidding are used for determining 10-year easement payments. The payment is calculated by taking 90 percent of the future value of CRP payments after 10 years and applying a discount rate to determine the "present value" of this amount. Adopting a 90 percent figure was an attempt to prevent undue competition between CRP and RIM Reserve. Or simply stated, RIM Reserve should be structured so that CRP funds are not prevented from being spent. The Minnesota Soil and Water Conservation Board, which administers the RIM Reserve, has employed a seven percent discount rate. This rate reflects the cost of bonding money to the state and investment opportunities over a 10-year period for landowners with a nominal amount of money.

The discount rate used in the present-value calculation can be viewed as the rate of interest looked at from a slightly different angle. After the future value of the CRP payments is calculated, an amount equaling a 10-year accumulation of seven percent interest is subtracted from it. To most landowners, a present-value concept is complicated and difficult to comprehend—a drawback—but the present-value basis of comparison is essential for a realistic solution to avoid competition with the federal program.

In addition to the 10-year easement, RIM Reserve also provides a permanent easement option under which a landowner agrees to retire cropland in perpetuity. For such, a landowner receives 70 percent of the equalized average estimated market value of tillable land in the township where the parcel is located. The logic behind the 70 percent figure is that poorer quality land is being retired. As with the 10-year easement, the landowner can choose between a lump-sum payment or four equal annual payments.

Although not implemented due to the restrictions imposed by the bonding appropriation, another provision of the legislation provided supplemental payments to programs, such as CRP or Federal Waterbank. This option was intended to allow a nominal amount of state funds to direct programs, such as CRP, by providing landowners with an incentive to submit bids on selected parcels and be more assured of an acceptable return. It was felt that supplemental payments might encourage skeptical landowners to enroll parcels important to state or local priorities. At the same time, CRP would not be facing competition; landowner interest may be enhanced. With respect to Federal Waterbank, supplemental payments would be used to "pick-up" expired contracts.

The farmer, therefore, has three options for enrolling land in a long-term conservation reserve program: the federal CRP and 10-year or permanent easements under the RIM reserve. Which program is the most attractive to a farmer? That depends on the farmer's long-term cropping interests, financial status, and several other variables.

The CRP provides an annual payment for each acre of eligible land based on a bid submitted by the farmer. If a farmer has a $60-per-acre bid accepted for a 40-acre parcel of land, he would be entitled to a $2,400 annual payment over the next 10 years.

If the farmer choose the RIM Reserve 10-year easement, he would receive a lump-sum payment of about $14,500 for his 40 acres, based on 90 percent of the $60-per-acre CRP payment, including the adjustment for a 7 percent discount rate.

But if a farmer opts for a permanent easement, he would be paid 70 percent of the equalized average estimated market value of tillable land in the township where the parcel is located. If for example, the estimated market value equals $700, the farmer would be entitled to $490 an acre, or $19,600 for the 40 acres. The most current land value data available is provided by the Minnesota Department of Revenue for annual periods. The current period covers July 1, 1986 to June 30, 1987 and reflects 1985 land values. With land values continuing to decline, it's no surprise that for much of Minnesota permanent easements based on 1985 land values offer attractive payments at this time.

While it could be argued that RIM Reserve payment rates don't reflect a concern for enrolling as much land as cheaply as possible, it must be noted that the broad program goals of wildlife habitat creation, water quality improvement, and soil erosion control justify higher payment rates.

Making the best choice between CRP, a 10-year RIM Reserve easement, or a permanent RIM Reserve easement depends upon current land values, rental rates, the farmer's current debt load, and other factors. Because land markets and the relationship between rental rates and market values vary considerably from location to location, the relative attractiveness of the three alternatives is likely to vary from county to county. For example, if rents are high compared to market value, the 10-year easement is probably a better option, the assumption being that CRP bid ceilings bear some relationship to rental rates.

Implementing the RIM plan

From the beginning, it was realized that implementing RIM Reserve would be a challenge. Because Minnesota is the first state to attempt such a program, there is no precedent to follow. Initiating RIM Reserve meant coordinating the efforts of the Soil and Water Conservation Board with the state's 91 conservation districts, the University of Minnesota Extension Service, the Department of Natural Resources, the Minnesota Pollution Control Agency, the U.S. Fish and Wildlife Service, the Agricultural Stabilization and Conservation Service, and the Soil Conservation Service.

In addition, the alliance of environmental, sportsmen, and farm groups that lobbied for RIM deserved a role in local implementation. To this end, local screening committees were established. Because soils, landscape characteristics, wildlife habitat, and potential benefits are site specific, local decision making and priority setting is essential. In cooperation with screening committees—a group of agency personnel, sportsmen, and local government officials—conservation districts are responsible for promotion, accepting applications, setting priorities, coordinating the review of proposed parcels, providing technical assistance for establishing vegetative cover, and performing administrative duties necessary to implement the program. Perhaps more than any feature of the program, screening committees offer an opportunity for conservation districts to take a pro-active approach to resource management. Screening committees with authority to develop a local course of action represent a grassroots effort that many rural sociologists would applaud. Research dealing with adoption diffusion theory has shown many times that a "top-down" approach stifles local creativity and promotes reactive local organizations.

Within provisions of administrative rules promulgated by the Soil and Water Conservation Board, screening committees have considerable discretion and decision-making authority. This philosophy is consistent with thoughts echoed by Nobel economist Theodore Schultz (7). Soil erosion is location-specific. Its technical and economic attributes vary widely, both within and between locations. Accordingly, a program—voluntary or mandatory—that does not allow flexibility will be less efficient than a flexible one.

Developing land eligibility criteria was another challenge and perhaps the most important if RIM Reserve was to meet its legislative objectives. To accomplish RIM's soil erosion control, water quality improvement, and wildlife habitat enhancement goals, soils with varying properties needed to be considered. Those soils include sandy, shallow, wet, and productive highly erodible soils. Moreover, legislative discussions focused on including land that was already adequately protected from erosion.

The CRP eligibility requirements generally exclude farmers who have controlled soil erosion. It can be argued that this administrative decision is defensible if CRP is viewed primarily as a soil conservation and erosion control program. With a broader goal of wildlife habitat enhancement, RIM Reserve regulations can legitimately accommodate landowners who have controlled soil losses. It is recognized that crop production—even when practiced in a soil-conserving manner—may not provide an optimum wildlife environment. Consequently, enrolling cropland parcels irrespective of management offers a greater opportunity to link private land to publicly owned parcels and, further, to riparian, wetland, or other favorable environments.

There is another reason for considering past soil conservation efforts of landowners. Considerable cropland is productive due only to soil-enhancing measures, such as crop rotation and residue management. Extra effort and investment may be needed to keep a marginal site in production. In today's economic climate, this is clearly not in the farmer's best interest. Although CRP may lack the administrative flexibility to employ this logic, it is justified in RIM Reserve.

A possible limitation to enrolling adequately protected cropland lies in the area of cost effectiveness. With respect to cost per ton of soil saved, RIM Reserve may not look too good, even with relatively low-cost, permanent vegetative cover. How does one measure water quality and wildlife habitat benefits in an environment confounded by financially strapped farmers who may be enrolling this land for strictly economic reasons? These issues beg for thoughtful and perhaps innovative analysis.

Furthermore, developing marginal land criteria for the RIM Reserve meant avoiding competition with the CRP program. After assessing the potential long-term funding possibilities of both CRP and RIM Reserve, policymakers established a 2.5-million-acre enrollment goal. These two points bore the conclusion that the land capability classification is too broad to be used as a classification system for RIM Reserve. As an illustration, if class III and class IVe, IVw, and IVs soils were combined with classes VI through VIII, the acreage would exceed 6.8 million acres. Using the land capability classification to arrive at the 2.5-million-acre goal would, therefore, preclude some subclasses and eliminate certain priority areas of the state. For example, droughty soils of outwash plains and glacial beach ridges located in central, west central, and northwestern Minnesota would be omitted if an erodible-weighted priority (e) were adopted.

Consequently, a search began for a new way to classify marginal cropland. Methods under development at the University of Minnesota Departments of Agricultural and Applied Economics and Soil Science were chosen for further review.

In 1983 Dr. William Larson and research assistant Francis Pierce of the Department of Soil Science developed a method of assessing soil productivity by calculating the suitability of soils as a rooting environment (4). In the view of many soil scientists and agronomists, the ability of a soil to provide a suitable rooting environment with nonrestrictive bulk density, adequate available water-holding capacity, and favorable pH is key to its productivity.

Soil productivity inputs are of two types: replaceable and nonreplaceable. Fertilizers and lime are examples of replaceable inputs. Usually, after a productive soil is cropped for a period of time without any external inputs, the yield of the crop starts to decline because of a reduced nutrient supply or a low pH. If the nutrients are replaced, lime is added, and the soil receives reasonable management, the soil may continue to produce crops at a high level for an indefinite period.

Limitations of plant rooting depth or a decline in available water-holding capacity are examples of nonreplaceable inputs. If some of the soil profile is removed by erosion, the desirable depth of soil may be reduced. Unless soil material beneath the rooting zone is as favorable as that on the surface, the total depth of rooting and water storage capacity will be reduced and yields will be limited in spite of fertilizer and lime additions.

Soils with favorable surface and subsoil characteristics could conceivably erode at significantly higher rates than soils with less favorable profiles and experience less loss of productivity. Soil conservation programs directed at those areas experiencing the highest rates of erosion may, therefore, be overprotecting some deep soils while underprotecting some shallow ones.

In quantifying these concepts, Larson and Pierce refined a model developed by soil scientists at the University of Missouri. Based upon the factors of available water capacity, bulk density, and pH, the productivity index (PI) model indexes a soil according to its suitability as an environment for plant roots. The factors are weighted by an idealized rooting distribution in 100 centimeters (39 inches) of soil. This depth was chosen because it corresponds with the base of common roots for deep-rooted crops, such as corn and soybeans. PI ranges from 0.0 to 1.0, with 1.0 representing a soil with an ideal rooting environment.

The approach uses easily obtainable inputs. It assumes a high degree of management, assesses only the change in nonreplaceable inputs as a result of erosion, and assesses long-term productive potential without consideration of annual fluctuations in yield caused by, for example, climate and plant differences. There is no estimation of the effects of gullying or loss of plant population due to erosion. Data needed to calculate PI and the changes in productivity due to erosion over time are obtained from the SCS-Soils-5 data base and the National Resources Inventory.

An associated concept is soil vulnerability, or the potential loss of favorable rooting zone (or productivity) as soil is eroded. A soil is said to be vulnerable if a loss in productivity is experienced as soil is eroded. To increase the utility of the vulnerability concept, University of Minnesota soil scientists incorporated factors representing the potential for erosion to occur. In other words, a highly vulnerable soil on level terrain in a water erosion-prone area may pose little risk to productivity because soil loss will be minimal. Combining the environmental factors, RKLS, from the univeral soil loss equation with vulnerability represents the resistance of a soil to productivity losses from water erosion. Wind erosion can be accommodated by incorporating the ICL factors from the wind erosion equation. In this manner all soils can be rated by their resistance to productivity losses from erosion. This resistance can be adapted to a 0.0 to 1.0 scale, called a resistance index (RI). A soil with an RI of 1.0 is extremely resistant to erosion-caused productivity losses. Productivity and resistivity indexes can be combined into a diagram, with PI values arranged in vertical, ascending order and RI values occupying a horizontal, increasing order. Some researchers suggest that this PI/RI diagram portrays a strategy for directing soil conservation and other farm program funds(6,8). Land parcels (or soil classes) can be characterized as falling into one of four quadrants according to each parcel's position along the

PI and RI gradients. If 50 percent PI and RI breakpoints are assumed, the diagram consists of four more or less equally sized subsets. The upper left quadrant might be thought of as having a risky (nonresistant) landscape with productive soils (NRP lands). The upper right quadrant comprises a nonrisky (resistant) landscape with productive soils (RP lands). The lower left quadrant comprises a risky landscape with nonproductive soils (NRNP lands). The lower right quadrant comprises a nonrisky landscape with nonproductive soils (RNP lands). The relationship of these categories to soil conservation and farm program policy is as follows:

1. *NRP lands:* These areas should be set aside from crop production because of the erosion risk, which would also maximize foregone crop production.

2. *RP lands:* Production should be encouraged because the land is productive and poses little risk to erosion. Public expenditure for erosion control practices is, therefore, minimized.

3. *NRNP lands:* These areas should be enrolled in CRP or the RIM Reserve because an erosion risk exists and the land is inherently unproductive, thus minimizing its usefulness for set-aside or crop production.

4. *RNP lands:* Program participation should be discouraged because the land poses few erosion risks and is not productive for set-aside purposes.

The size of the respective "block" can be adjusted according to program funding or acreage goals. For example, if limited funds were available for a conservation reserve, a 25 percent breakpoint could be used. This narrows the zone of nonproductive/nonresistant lands, thus focusing attention on more critical areas. Additional lands would then be available for other categories. A 25 percent criterion was adopted for RIM Reserve. This breakpoint yielded about 2.5 million acres. National Resources Inventory data and environmental factors from the erosion equations were used to generate the data necessary to establish the PI and RI quadrants and associated soils and acreages.

The NRI was performed at a sample frequency designed to be accurate to the county level for much of Minnesota. Of the more than 16,000 primary sampling units, a majority were concentrated in counties with large cropland acreages. Numbers of sampling units ranged from less than 100 in heavily forested counties to more than 200 in intensively cropped counties. Consequently, some soils were missed even in heavily sampled counties.

Values for RI, RKLS, and ICL are as variable as the landscape and associated soils. For example, if NRI points were located in a cropland field with short unsheltered distances, even an unproductive fine sand might have RI approaching 1.0—resistant to erosion. Conversely, the same soil at locations with longer, unsheltered distances may be nonresistant to erosion and, therefore, eligible. The RI concept is more accurate if used on a multicounty or state basis. For these reasons, local knowledge of soils and landscapes must be reflected in a revision process. The conservation districts are provided an opportunity to develop a local eligible soil mapping unit list based on a proposed list developed by the state board in cooperation with the University of Minnesota Department of Soil Science and the Soil Conservation Service. Conservation districts are encouraged to solicit outside opinion in the development of the local soils list. To maintain consistency among counties, the state board approves all local lists.

The PI and RI concepts are the basis for defining marginal agricultural lands in the adopted RIM Reserve rules. Marginal agricultural land is defined in the rule as "land with cropland soils that are inherently unproductive for agricultural crop production and subject to significant potential soil productivity loss from erosion." The PI portion of this definition is referenced in the rule as inherently unproductive, which means that "the soil properties of available water capacity, bulk density and pH in the uppermost 100 centimeters of a soil, are present in a manner such that an unfavorable rooting environment exists." Significant potential soil productivity loss refers to the RI concept. This is defined in the rule as a loss that "may occur in a short time unless management measures are initiated to control soil erosion. The method of calculation combines the rating of a soil as a rooting environment with landscape characteristics that represent erosion potential."

A review of land deemed eligible by these definitions reveals some erodible(e), droughty(s), and wet(w) soils. Wet soils require special consideration. As they relate to PI and RI, wet soils are marginal not because of excess water but because they have a poor rooting environment in terms of bulk density or pH. Furthermore, undrained wet soils have probably not been cropped consistently enough to qualify for the RIM Reserve, which requires that enrolled land must have been cropped in two of five years during the period from 1981 to 1985.

Relating eligible soils to proposed parcels is relatively easy in counties with published soil surveys. At locations where detailed soils information is not available, a qualified soil scientist must classify the soils of proposed parcels to at least the family level of taxonomy. With this information, eligibility of proposed parcels can be determined by comparing the soils to those on an area mapping unit legend.

Although this discussion has focused on the soils component of marginal lands, it must be emphasized that many other factors have a bearing on parcel selection. Fisheries, wildlife, and water quality considerations must be included in parcel selection decisions made at the local level. To alleviate concerns that the inherent inaccuracy of NRI data when used at a sub-county level may result in unfair allocations to conservation districts, RIM Reserve funding was not based solely on eligible soil acreage. Other factors, such as the extent of lakes, streams, or wildlife management areas, were also considered.

In summary, the marginal land classification system developed for the RIM Reserve has the following advantages over land capability classification and rate of soil loss methods:

► The extent of eligible soils can be adjusted according to acreage goals; in so doing, most types of soils, landscapes, and geographic acres can be accommodated; but the method always separates the least resistant and least productive lands, whichever criterion is used.

► Soil loss calculations are unnecessary.

► Because eligible soils are provided, advance determination of eligible areas is minimized.

There are also disadvantages:

► New methods represent a departure from time-honored procedures.

► The PI and RI method might be viewed as too complicated and therefore, dismissed for lack of understanding.

► Inherent characteristics of NRI data may create interpretation problems, particularly in those counties with a small cropland base.

► Some may argue that too much reliance has been placed on accuracy of the SCS-Soils-5 data base.

The disadvantages are manageable if local users are given an opportunity to revise the soil lists on the basis of their knowledge about the landscape and soil. As mentioned earlier, this opportunity is available.

The comprehensive goals of the RIM Reserve warranted a new approach to classifying marginal cropland. The method described shows promise in meeting the challenges of RIM Reserve.

This new approach to classifying cropland creates opportunities to further implement soil productivity and vulnerability concepts. Wildlife habitat programs could, for example, be developed for soils in the resistant, non-productive category by focusing on sites with desirable features, such as poor drainage. Larson and associates (3) discussed the utility of productivity and vulnerability indices in targeting state and local soil conservation efforts. A number of applications are possible: redefinition of T values, establishment of planning horizons based on a local consensus concerning allowable soil productivity losses, and incorporation of off-site concerns into the decision-making process. A recent Ohio report (9) demonstrates the local demand for additional methods to promote and quantify the effect of soil erosion on productivity.

Some additional RIM reserve specifics

The marginal cropland eligible under the RIM Reserve rule must meet additional criteria, which require the land to be owned by the applicant on January 1, 1985; at least five acres in size, or a whole field as defined by the Agricultural Stabilization and Conservation Service; not set-aside, enrolled, or diverted under another federal or state government program; physically possible to crop; in agricultural crop production for at least two years during the period 1981 to 1985; and less than 20 percent of the landowner's total agricultural acreage in the state.

At least 50 percent of the easement acreage must consist of marginal cropland. An additional 50 percent of higher quality cropland may be included if beneficial to resource protection or for efficient recording of the land description. It is possible for a farmer to enroll land in both CRP and RIM, although not the same acreage. Approved landowners will receive up to $75 per acre to establish perennial grass-legume or native grass cover. An additional amount up to $75 per acre will be provided for tree planting as required by the conservation plan agreement.

Actions prohibited on the enrolled acres include crop production, alteration of wildlife habitat, grazing, and spraying with chemicals or mowing, except to comply with noxious weed control laws.

Additional landowner requirements prohibit the converting of other land owned or leased by the landowner that is currently supporting natural vegetation to cropland during the term of the easement. Thus, under the provisions of a perpetual easement, sodbusting and swampbusting are prohibited forever.

At the option of the Minnesota commissioner of agriculture and with the concurrance of the landowner, a 10-year easement may be renewed for an additional period of 10 years or the temporary easement may be relinquished in favor of a permanent easement. Payment rates may be adjusted at that time based on the condition of the established cover, conservation practices, and land values.

A recent, significant U.S. Department of Agriculture ruling provides acreage-base protection for farmers by allowing enrolled RIM Reserve acreage to be designated as conserving use. There is no pro-rate reduction of bases as there is with the CRP. USDA indicated the favorable ruling reflected a desire to see states adopt conservation reserve programs. This should be, in itself, an incentive for many farmers to participate (2).

The implications of RIM

The RIM Reserve means different things to the groups and people who supported it in the legislature. RIM owes its existence to the strong grassroots support it received from a coalition of organizations concerned with farming, wildlife habitat, and environmental quality. In fact, a legislative alliance called the RIM Coalition, comprised of hunting, fishing, and conservation organization leaders, is providing support and lobbying efforts to keep long-term funding proposals moving forward. More important for conservation districts, a strong lobby and important relationships were developed. In the past, divergent groups supported conservation and resource programs, but for different reasons. Now they are working together in a mutually rewarding effort.

To conservationists, the program is a chance to reduce pollution of Minnesota streams and lakes caused by sedimentation and nutrient runoff. To environmentalists, it is a chance to regain for wildlife the values of wetlands and undisturbed vegetative cover. To outdoor enthusiasts, RIM means better recreation. To resort owners and other tourist-oriented businesses, it means improved trade. To farmers, it is both a source of income at a time when many of them desperately need it and a source of support for soil and water conservation. Moreover, it may make farmers aware of the potential financial benefits of enhancing wildlife populations for willing-to-pay urban dwellers.

To the Soil and Conservation Board, RIM is a major step toward accomplishing land treatment goals. RIM provides another tool in the implementation of state soil and water conservation policy and an important link to federal policy. Thus, rather than relying solely on more traditional techniques, an opportunity is achieved to prove that cost-effective conservation involves preventative approaches rather than remedial or corrective measures (5).

Although the RIM legislation has been adopted by the Council of State Governments as a national model, it may not be universally applicable in its present form. Nevertheless, the coalition-building necessary for its passage and the concepts developed for implementation should prove useful to states considering similar efforts.

REFERENCES

1. Batie, S.S. 1984. *Soil erosion: Crisis in America's croplands?* The Conservation Foundation, Washington, D.C. pp. 116-117.
2. Hoag, D.L., and D.L. Young. 1985. *Toward effective land retirement legislation.* Journal of Soil and Water Conservation 40: 462-466.
3. Larson, G.A., F.J. Pierce, and L.J. Winkelman. 1984. *Soil productivity and vulnerability indices for erosion control programs.* In *Erosion and Soil Productivity: Proceedings of the National Symposium on Erosion and Soil Productivity.* American Society of Agricultural Engineers, St. Joseph, Michigan. pp. 243-253.
4. Pierce, F.J., W.E. Larson, R.H. Dowdy, and W.A.P. Graham. 1983. *Productivity of soils: Assessing long-term changes due to erosion.* Journal of Soil and Water Conservation 38: 39-44.
5. Raup, P.M. 1984. *Discussion to a land use commentary.* In B.C. English, J.A. Maetzold, B.R. Holding, and E.O. Heady [editors] *Future Agricultural Technology and Resource Conservation.* Iowa State University Press, Ames. pp. 128-131.
6. Runge, C.F., W.E. Larson, and G. Roloff. 1986. *Using productivity measures to target conservation programs: A comparative analysis.* Journal of Soil and Water Conservation 41: 45-49.
7. Schultz, T.W. 1982. *The dynamics of soil erosion in the U.S.: A critical view.* In Proceedings, Conference on Soil Conservation. Agricultural Council of America, Washington, D.C.
8. Taff, S., and C.F. Runge. 1986. *Supply control, conservation and budget restraint: Conflicting instruments in the 1985 Farm Bill.* Staff paper series P. 86-33. Department of Agricultural and Applied Economics, University of Minnesota, St. Paul.
9. U.S. Department of Agriculture, Soil Conservation Service. 1985. *Graph PI model special inventory.* Fiscal year 1985 Report. Columbus, Ohio.

10

A framework for state soil conservation program initiatives

James L. Arts

The idea that a state could and should have a strong soil conservation progam is relatively new. The soil conservation program initiated in the 1930s largely bypassed the states in favor of a federal-local system. States were asked only to adopt enabling legislation that authorized creation of local conservation districts and to create a state-level committee to coordinate district activities. Federal officials and agencies, working through local committees, controlled most of the money for cost-sharing (Agricultural Conservation Program of the Agricultural Stabilization and Conservation Service) and technical assistance (Soil Conservation Service).

Of late this model has been breaking down, and now it seems reasonable to believe that a major break from the traditional system is not only likely but justified. There are several reasons why states are becoming stronger relative to federal agencies:

▶ The impact of highly critical General Accounting Office and other reviews of federal programs (*13,14*).

▶ The decline in federal funding for soil conservation and other programs resulting from changing federal priorities.

▶ The strengthened role of state water quality programs (as a result of Public Law 92-500 and subsequent laws) and the recognition that soil erosion must be controlled if water quality goals are to be met.

▶ The recognition of the need to use state land use authority to deal with some soil erosion, nonpoint-source, and groundwater pollution problems.

Critical reviews of federal programs. Beginning with the 1977 GAO report(*13*) *To Protect Tomorrow's Food Supply, Soil Conservation Needs Priority Attention*, there has been completed a series of reviews critical of SCS and ASCS performance. The reports have charged that these U.S. Department of Agriculture agencies have fallen short in a number of program areas, including the primary charge that the agencies have not targeted technical and financial assistance to the areas with the highest soil erosion rates. These criticisms of the USDA agencies, along with the agencies' unimpressive record during the Resources Conservation Act process in the 1970s, tended to undercut confidence in their ability to undertake innovative program responsibilities. This has provided an opportunity for a stronger state role. Countering this trend is the enactment of the important conservation title provisions in the Food Security Act of 1985, which should help give federal agencies a renewed sense of mission.

Decline in federal funding. Federal soil conservation budgets have declined somewhat in recent years and, in constant dollar terms, have declined enormously compared to budgets in the 1930s. There is a chance this trend will change, but little likelihood that it will change dramatically. State soil conservation budgets have increased and may continue to do so. Funding by state and local governments has increased from $176 million in 1981 to $276 million in 1985. Presumably, along with this money will come greater influence.

State water quality programs. Another independent but concurrent development has also tended to promote stronger state involvement. This development is the 1972 and subsequent amendments to the Federal Water Pollution Control Act that require state water quality planning, including development of nonpoint-source pollution control programs. Wisconsin has developed a major watershed program intended to meet nonpoint-source control objectives (*7*). In some watersheds most of the effort and cost-share funding are directed toward soil conservation measures. Combined annual expenditures for nonpoint-source pollution control and soil conservation by state and county governments in Wisconsin now exceed the SCS and ASCS budgets for technical assistance and cost-sharing for similar purposes.

State land use power. Soil erosion must be controlled if water quality goals are to be met, and it does not appear likely that soil erosion will be controlled adequately without some exercise of state land use control authority. Under our federal system, states have retained authority for establishing land use policy and for implementing land use controls, while the federal government has asserted responsibility for water policy. For some time it has been recognized that it would be necessary to join federal water policy with state land policy to ensure that the necessary measures to protect the water are installed on the land (*11*). For the most part states have delegated the exercise of land use control authority to local units of government. Even in cases where the goal is water quality protection, land use regulations are often enacted and administered by local governments, as they are in Wisconsin under the state's shoreland zoning program.

Changing patterns of organization

Trends. The dramatic early success of the national soil conservation program was due in part to the superb organizational system established in the 1930s that emphasized a federal-local relationship. In that time an intense national effort was needed along with substantial local participation. A strong state role would only have complicated program responsibilities. At the local level, conservation districts—special purpose units of state government—provided the uniformity, focus, and energy that no general purpose unit of government could then provide.

Now, a half century later, changing governmental roles and natural resource issues indicate that a different governmental system may be more effective than the one established in the 1930s. Important current developments and trends include:

► Recognition of the interrelationship between agricultural and environmental issues, including soil conservation, groundwater and surface water pollution, pesticide regulation, and farmland protection.

► Increasing state program activity in these areas.

► Decreasing reliance on special-purpose units of government and growing delegation of responsibility to county government.

► Increasing likelihood that soil conservation programs will include regulatory components.

The trends also suggest that the special district concept for soil conservation programs may not be as appropriate today as it was in the 1930s and 1940s. Wisconsin's organizational approach is designed to reflect these trends.

Wisconsin's soil conservation organization: County level. No doubt there are many ways that the federal, state, and local governments can organize themselves to achieve an effective, efficient, and accountable program;

what works well in one state may not work well in other states. The system used in Wisconsin is an example of a state that has attempted to deal with current developments in the agricultural and natural resource arenas.

Wisconsin's soil conservation organization is somewhat different from that of any other state because local soil conservation responsibilities have been delegated to the county, operating through its land conservation committee, rather than to conservation districts or other types of natural resource districts. Wisconsin's soil and water conservation districts were abolished by the legislature in 1982.

This change was intended to:

► Place soil conservation authority in a general-purpose unit of government with broad authority, including taxation power.

► Improve coordination between the soil conservation function and other county-level natural resource program functions, especially those administered by the planning and zoning committee.

► Improve coordination between the county soil conservation function and the ASCS county committee.

► Improve the capability of state and county governments to exercise soil and water conservation program leadership.

The delegation of the soil conservation function to county government reflects a belief that soil and water conservation districts, as special-purpose units of state government, were not adequately addressing soil conservation issues (2) and were not likely to do so in the future. Recently, a major soil conservation study concluded that "increased involvement of county governments may be the most critical need in improving state and local soil conservation programs" (1).

Placing soil conservation responsibility directly into county government has improved the Wisconsin program, and there is potential for further improvement. On the other hand, the improvements have not been dramatic, and most counties have not moved energetically to increase substantially soil conservation funding, enact regulations, broaden the base of participation or interest in soil conservation, or improve coordination with related natural resource programs. There have been improvements in these areas, but they have not been spectacular.

The land conservation committees are required, by statute, to include at least two members of the county's committee on agriculture and extension education and the chairperson of the ASCS county committee. In addition to these required members, the county board may appoint any number of additional county board members and up to two people who are not on the county board. Most LCCs have five or six members, but the range is from four to nine.

In addition to these voting members, the statutes require the county to designate a member from other county committees that have responsibilities in natural resource management to serve as an advisor to the LCC. The LCC may also invite any agency with which it has a memorandum of understanding (such as SCS) to designate a representative to advise the LCC.

The purpose of this structure is to expand the committee's range of interests and improve coordination among county and federal agencies. Especially noteworthy is the placement of the chairperson of the ASCS county committee on the LCC. This is intended to provide a direct link between the two county-level committees responsible for soil conservation activity. It seems generally agreed that this interlocking membership requirement has significantly improved the working relationship between county government and the ASCS county committee.

Most counties have created a land conservation department to provide an administrative home for LCC staff. In some cases the LCC staff has been integrated into other county departments. Such integration can have several benefits, including improved efficiency, more convenience for the public, more coordinated use of computerized land information systems, and improved coordination of related programs.

LCC staff numbers and capabilities vary substantially from county to county. The SCS continues to provide technical assistance under an agreement with each LCC, but the primary responsibility for program direction and administration is shifting to the county. This contrasts with the historically strong administrative role SCS has assumed in many soil and water conservation districts.

Wisconsin's soil conservation organization: State level. At the state level the Wisconsin Department of Agriculture, Trade and Consumer Protection administers the soil conservation program. This department also administers farmland preservation, animal waste management, pesticide and fertilizer regulation, and agricultural impact statement programs. An eight-member Land Conservation Board has certain responsibilities for many of these programs, especially for the Farmland Preservation Program. Serving on the Land Conservation Board are the heads of the Department of Natural Resources; Department of Agriculture, Trade and Consumer Protection; and Department of Administration as well as three members of county land conservation committees and two appointees of the governor (2). This diverse board membership contributes to improved program coordination.

New program initiatives

There are many new state soil conservation programs around the country. Two new programs in Wisconsin—The Soil Erosion Control Program and the Farmland Preservation Program—have major soil conservation objectives. Another, the Nonpoint-Source Water Pollution Abatement Program, has a water quality objective but funds many soil conservation measures in order to achieve water quality objectives. Still others deal with animal waste or pesticide regulation and have some relationship to soil conservation.

Soil erosion control program. The Soil Erosion Control Program, created in 1982, was intended to address concerns about the approach to soil conservation criticized by General Accounting Office reviews of federal soil conservation programs. The heart of the GAO concern was that program efforts were not targeted to the most severe erosion areas and that agency staff did not aggressively seek out landowners with the most severe soil erosion. To meet this concern, the state needed an inventory of soil erosion rates and a systematic plan to deal with excessive erosion. The county soil erosion plans are intended to provide both. Fifty-five of Wisconsin's 72 counties have been identified as priority counties and are required to prepare soil erosion plans. A few counties have completed their plans; the remainder are slated to have plans completed during 1987.

Soil erosion control plans have several purposes, including:

▶ Indentification of high erosion areas within a county. Many county plans identify erosion rates on a farm-by-farm or even field-by-field basis.

▶ Increased awareness of soil erosion within the county. This is done through public meetings, information provided through news media, and notices to individual farmers.

▶ Development of a coordinated action plan to meet soil erosion control goals.

The state has paid up to 50 percent of the cost of preparing plans. When the plans are completed in 1987, the state will have provided about $800,000 and counties about $1 million for completing the plans.

This is a substantial investment, but it is a relatively small part of the current and future total annual public expenditures for soil and water conservation. In Wisconsin the current annual total is about $15 million, including $4.7 million for the Agricultural Conservation Program, $5 million for Soil Conservation Service technical assistance, $3.8 million from county appropriations, and $1.5 million from state appropriations. Assuming that, on the average, about 60 percent of this amount, or about $9 million, is spent on soil erosion control, then the $1.8 million for planning is 20 percent of the annual budget for soil erosion and just 2 percent of the projected 10-year soil erosion budget, assuming current spending levels continue. The soil erosion plans will need some updating, but are intended to be long-range plans directed toward meeting the "T by 2000" goal. If they help to target resources to areas of greatest need, as they are expected to, the investment in planning will easily be worth the cost.

The process of preparing the plans and the information the plans are generating have great value. The Wisconsin Department of Agriculture, Trade and Consumer Protection, in a recently completed report (*15*), provided reasons for the usefulness of these plans:

▶ The plans have identified cropland erosion rates. The level of detail varies, but all counties will have a general inventory for the entire county and a field-by-field inventory for high-priority areas. In preparing this inventory, counties collect and analyze a great mass of data relating to soil erosion. Some of these data existed in bits and pieces in different offices, agencies, and documents, but most did not exist at all. Counties have put this information together to develop an integrated view of erosion within the county. These plans represent the first time this documentation of the problem has ever been assembled. By analyzing all existing and proposed programs, counties have been able to prepare plans that are particularly suited to the physical, economic, political, and social conditions of each county. Such localized plans—which use the most appropriate features of each relevant governmental program and often develop new ways of accomplishing erosion control—have the best chance for local acceptance and effective implementation. This information will be used for many purposes, including targeting of cost-sharing programs. This will help to mitigate the problem of lack of information, which was identified in a survey by USDA's Agricultural Research Service and Economic Research Service as a primary reason USDA funds were not targeted to the most serious erosion areas (*9*).

▶ The establishment of a specific goal and interim goals for soil erosion control, and the development of plans to meet these goals, have forced a reassessment of the entire erosion control delivery framework. For many counties, a substantial reordering of priorities, including adding staff to work with farmers with erosion problems, more active involvement of the land conservation committee in erosion control issues, and a greater financial commitment from agencies, will be necessary if erosion control goals are to be reached. This change in the way soil conservation problems are handled—a switch from reacting to farmer-initiated requests for assistance to identifying problem areas and actively promoting erosion control in them—is necessary if goals are to be reached. Some county plans have been better at realizing this needed change in basic philosophy than others, but all have indicated they will approach erosion control more systematically and aggressively than in the past.

► The establishment of county-level soil conservation goals that must, at a minimum, meet the state's "T by 2000" goal has focused attention and resources toward activities that have the greatest potential for soil erosion control. Moreover, counties are using the plan to coordinate all soil conservation program resources, whether from federal, state, or county sources. In some cases, it will be possible to reach state and county goals by redirecting available resources.

► The plans have served as catalysts for developing computerized land information systems, which integrate detailed multi-year farm plans, erosion inventory information, zoning information, and a digitized soil survey, and provide tabular or graphic displays of information. Some of these systems were not developed solely for erosion control, but the erosion control planning process, using information from different sources, has greatly accelerated their adoption. Once in place, they will enable conservation offices to work with greater efficiency, allowing more time to be spent in the field installing erosion control practices and less in the office doing paperwork. These systems will also help to improve the capability of monitoring progress toward accomplishment of soil conservation objectives.

Farmland preservation program. Wisconsin's Farmland Preservation Program provides income tax credits to farmers who protect farmland from development for nonagricultural uses. Credits are available if either (a) the farmland is in an area zoned for exclusive agricultural use or (b) the farmer signs a 10-to 25-year contract with the state to protect the land from development.

All farmers who receive tax credits must meet soil conservation standards established and enforced by county land conservation committees under guidelines established by the Wisconsin Land Conservation Board (*16*). In 1985 about 20,000 farmers received tax credits totaling more than $34 million per year. This number was expected to increase to about 22,000 farmers receiving credits of about $40 million in 1986. The Department of Agricultural, Trade and Consumer Protection estimates that at least

25,000 farmers will be receiving tax credits when the soil conservation requirements are fully implemented in 1988. Farmland Preservation Program participation is expected to continue to increase, thus protecting more land from development and controlling soil erosion on that land.

Prior to 1986, farmers who received tax credits because they signed a long-term contract to protect farmland were required to have and comply with a soil conservation plan. This requirement, in effect since 1977, forced county soil conservation staff to enforce these requirements and to develop efficient techniques for doing so (6). The new cross-compliance requirements, enacted in 1985, substantially expand the number of farmers affected and will require a better system for monitoring compliance. This necessity is leading to the invention of streamlined techniques for monitoring compliance. State and county soil conservation staff are currently working with USDA staff to coordinate these state cross-compliance requirements with the federal conservation compliance requirements in the Food Security Act of 1985.

The addition of soil conservation requirements to the Farmland Preservation Program expanded the multiple-purpose nature of that program. It now has a comprehensive soil erosion control objective as well as three previously existing objectives:

► Property tax relief, through a formula that provides higher tax credits for higher property taxes, up to a certain point.

► Agricultural land preservation, through long-term contracts and local exclusive agricultural use zoning.

► Family farm preservation because tax relief is targeted toward medium-size family farms.

The remaining Wisconsin agenda. An expanded state soil conservation role is desirable, but substituting state or county program direction for that of federal administration will not accomplish much without program redirection. Some of this redirection is happening in Wisconsin and some is not.

In building on recent accomplishments, Wisconsin agencies will need to consider how several areas can be improved:

Targeting. Whether soil conservation programs should be targeted should no longer be a debatable issue; the relevant questions now relate to targeting criteria, standards, and goals. These are not simple questions, and their answers very likely will involve use of new standards to replace T values and more sophisticated models to replace the USLE (10).

Program coordination. Coordination of soil erosion, pesticide and fertilizer management, and water quality programs will be more difficult in some states than in others, depending upon whether the state is presently doing much in these other areas and upon relationships among agricultural and environmental agencies in the state.

A consistent policy for these program areas is important so that maximum efficiency be achieved and so that practices promoted in one program are not counterproductive for another. Some states are approaching a crisis because of groundwater pollution from agricultural sources. In Wisconsin some progress has been achieved in coordinating these programs through the placement of soil conservation, animal waste management, pesticide regulation, farmland preservation, and fertilizer storage regulations in the Agricultural Resource Management Division of the Department of Agriculture, Trade and Consumer Protection. Additional work is needed to reduce agriculture's adverse impacts on the environment in a way that improves farm profitability (4).

Regulatory programs. Regulatory programs have not been welcomed by the traditional soil conservation establishment, and they are no panacea. The words of regulatory statutes do not leap off the pages of the law books to hold soil in place. Nevertheless, regulations are a part of modern agricultural life for milk production, pesticide use, animal health, and even noxious weed control. They may be needed to promote the credibility of soil conservation programs, especially when there are off-site damages from soil erosion. Even if there are no off-site damages, a credible argument could be made that the state has a public trust responsibility for the soil, as it does for water.

No doubt the federal government could devise some means of adopting direct soil erosion regulations, or forcing the states to do so, through use of its powers to tax and spend, to regulate interstate commerce, or to promote the general welfare. But we may safely assume federal inaction on this point and must recognize the need to look to state and local government's use of their police power to regulate excessive soil erosion (8).

Cost-effectiveness. Cost-effectiveness has not appeared to concern federal agencies much, at least not until very recently. Even now, USDA economists report that the benefits of erosion control are often substantially less than the outlays that have financed these control measures (12). It is possible to be skeptical about the narrow criteria used in economic analyses and still recognize that many soil erosion control funds have not been wisely invested. There have been too many expensive structures and too many practices installed on land that has little potential to erode to conclude that a targeted approach using low-cost conservation measures is not needed.

The early results from a study in Pepin County, Wisconsin, illustrate this point. In that county SCS, working with the county and town governments, offered a modest $3.00 per acre to farmers whose lands met soil conservation standards. Many farmers' lands already met the standards, of course, but many others did not. Even though virtually no cost-sharing was offered, a high percentage of farmers not in compliance undertook the conservation measures needed, usually low-cost management practices, to receive the $3.00 per acre per year credit. The lesson appears to be that farmers often do have the ability to implement practices needed to control erosion, and they will do so with cost-effective practices if an effective motivational strategy can be devised. This conclusion is supported by a recently completed study that the availability of cost-sharing has little influence on whether a farmer installs conservation measures (5).

County staff capabilities. Wisconsin's soil conservation and water quality programs are administered at the county level by the staff of the county land conservation departments. These staff people are important government workers in the soil conservation system because they work directly with the landowners, whose management practices and decisions will determine whether soil erosion is to be adequately controlled. To be effective, county staff must have high degrees of skill in many areas, including project management, interpersonal relations, and technical soil conservation skills. In Wisconsin, there are not now an adequate number of county staff people who have these skills. Resolution of this problem will require additional state funding, better training for county staff, and better state and county long-range planning. If this happens, counties can better predict long-term staff needs and make commitments to provide adequate staff, with state financial help.

Improved coordination between research and program development components. Useful and sophisicated research is now being done on some essential aspects of soil erosion policy. This research includes work on the cost effectiveness of soil conservation measures, the effects of soil erosion on crop productivity, conservation tillage, and other areas. Much more work is needed on these and other topics. As important as completion of needed research is the use of research findings in the policymaking and program implementation process. Policy research and recommendations by the American Farmland Trust (1) have been influential in recent federal soil conservation policy and are superb examples of a useful relationship between research (of a policy analysis type) and program development.

Wisconsin soil conservation agencies have recognized the need to coordinate research with program development and implementation by establishing a Council for Soil and Water Conservation Research and Education, composed of representatives of the University of Wisconsin system; Department of Agriculture, Trade and Consumer Protection; and the Land Conservation Board. The council was established in 1982, but its performance has, regrettably, been inadequate. Council members are now evaluating whether the council should continue and, if so, in what form. The council has largely served as a forum for reports and discussion; it has not been used effectively to evaluate research needs, track progress of research proposals and projects, and influence program development.

Future federal-state relations

State initiatives will help rejuvenate the soil conservation establishment, but federal action will also be important. In particular, successful implementation of the soil conservation provisions of the Food Security Act of 1985 are essential if federal, state, and county soil erosion goals are to be met in Wisconsin. Fortunately, the federal soil conservation initiatives are similar to Wisconsin's cross-compliance requirements. Federal and Wisconsin state agencies are now working to develop a joint systematic implementation program. Data developed during the county soil erosion control planning process will help to target the implementation efforts and will also help to locate highly erodible land for the sodbuster program.

Wisconsin has not yet had much success with the Conservation Reserve Program; only about 80,000 acres have entered the CRP as of 1986. This number is expected to increase as farmers' recognition of other soil erosion control program requirements increases, but some additional state attention, such as that given by Minnesota in the Reinvest in Minnesota (RIM) program, may be needed to reach optimal CRP participation levels. In March 1986 the Wisconsin legislature enacted two modest inducements to CRP participation: local assessors were directed to consider the change in property value resulting from enrollment of the land in the CRP and a state tree planting program was authorized that provides free trees for planting on land in the CRP or on highly erodible land identified in a completed county soil erosion control plan. However, only a million trees were provided for the program.

The federal conservation for credit or easement for debt exchange program is a highly promising marriage of farm debt and conservation objectives. The easement concept is now being studied by University of

Wisconsin Extension staff and by conservation organizations.

There are other vital federal roles, such as research. Development of the universal soil loss equation was of great value to soil conservationists, even though the USLE is not applicable for such needs as predicting off-site damages. But a good deal more research is needed on the relationship of soil erosion to cropland productivity, on models suitable for use by administrative agencies in soil erosion and water quality programs, and on the development of agricultural systems that reduce input costs and environmental damage but retain adequate productivity and profitability.

To facilitate use of federal research and program information, federal agencies should consider developing a communication link between the central federal office, ordinarily in Washington, D.C., and the state soil conservation agency, rather than using the more cumbersome and haphazard method of depending upon the state-level office of the federal agency to communicate new program initiatives, research results, and other matters.

Conclusion

Wisconsin has developed a good example of the expanded soil conservation role being assumed by states. This trend may rejuvenate the soil conservation establishment and, along with important soil conservation provisions in the Food Security Act of 1985, direct soil conservation efforts toward better targeted, cost-effective, and coordinated directions.

Organizational changes at the state and county levels in Wisconsin are intended to improve program coordination and to result in stronger program administration capabilities. County government has been delegated major planning implementation responsibility, and state-level responsibilities have been expanded and coordinated.

Wisconsin's Soil Erosion Control Program is intended to overcome some shortcomings of previous soil conservation programs by providing better information on soil erosion rates and locations and by targeting resources into these areas. The vehicle for achieving these objectives is the county soil erosion control planning process, to be completed in Wisconsin counties by the end of 1987.

Soil conservation cross-compliance requirements in the Wisconsin Farmland Preservation Program preceded similiar requirements in the federal Food Security Act of 1985 and are compatible with the federal requirements. By 1988, about 25,000 Wisconsin farmers will be receiving tax credits under the Farmland Preservation Program and meeting soil conservation standards established by the state Land Conservation Board.

These developments represent an important change in approach to soil conservation programs by strengthening state and county administrative capabilities; targeting resources into high erosion areas in a more cost-effective manner; integrating soil conservation programs, land preservation programs, and related resource protection activities; and implementing a quasi-regulatory approach through cross-compliance requirements. Implementing these initiatives will be challenging, but they appear to be conceptually sound and in harmony with major trends in federal-state relations and program approaches to soil erosion problems.

REFERENCES

1. American Farmland Trust. 1984. *Soil conservation in America: What do we have to lose?.* Washington, D.C.
2. Arts, James L. 1984. *Coordinating soil conservation programs; The Wisconsin approach.* Journal of Soil and Water Conservation, 39(6):354 356.
3. Arts, James L., et al. 1982. *Soil erosion—the next crisis?* Wisconsin Law Review: 535-626.
4. Cook, Ken. 1985. *Agriculture and conservation: What prospects for a merger into regenerative production systems?* Soil Conservation Society of America, Ankeny, Iowa.
5. Flory, Bruce Earl. 1986. *The impact of farm financial stress on investment in soil conservation.* Ph.D. Dissertation. University of Wisconsin, Madison.
6. Johnson, Leonard C., and James A. Johnson. 1982. *Cross-compliance in Wisconsin's farmland preservation program.* Journal of Soil and Water Conservation 37(3):141-142.
7. Konrad, John G., James S. Bauman, and Susan E. Berquist. 1985. *Nonpoint pollution control: The Wisconsin experience.* Journal of Soil and Water Conservation 40(1):55-61.
8. Myers, Peter C. 1986. *Nonpoint-source pollution control: The USDA Position.* Journal of Soil and Water Conservation 41(3):156-158.
9. Nielson, James. 1986. *Conservation targeting: Success or failure?* Journal of Soil and Water Conservation 41(2):70-76.
10. Nowak, Peter J., John Timmons, John Carlson, and Randy Miles. 1985. *Economic and social perspectives on T values relative to soil erosion and crop productivity.* In R.F. Follett and B.A. Stewart [editors] *Soil Erosion and Crop Productivity.* American Society of Agronomy, Madison, Wisconsin. pp. 119-132.
11. Runge, Carlisle P. 1976 *Land management institutional design for water quality objectives* In *Best Management Practices for Non-Point Source Pollution Control Seminar.* U.S. Environmental Protection Agency, Washington, D.C.
12. U.S. Department of Agriculture, Economic Research Service. 1986. *An economic analysis of USDA erosion control programs: A new perspective.* Washington, D.C.
13. U.S. General Accounting Office. 1977. *To protect tomorrow's food supply, soil conservation needs priority attention.* Washington, D.C.
14. U.S. General Accounting Office. 1983. *Agriculture's soil conservation programs miss full potential in the fight against soil erosion.* Washington, D.C.
15. Wisconsin Department of Agriculture, Trade and Consumer Protection. 1986. *Report on Wisconsin's soil erosion control program.* Madison.
16. Wisconsin Land Conservation Board. 1985. *Guidelines for soil and water conservation requirements in the farmland preservation program.* Madison.

11

Intergovernmental relations: Trends and opportunities

John B. Braden

Soil and water conservation programs are well preserved examples of New Deal government architecture: set on bedrock populism, designed in the Keynesian style, and constructed of federal subsidies. A half-century after completion, the bedrock seems unstable, Keynesian designs are passe, and federal subsidies are under fire.

The aim here is to explore renovations of soil and water conservation institutions. The emphasis is on emerging state and local soil and water conservation initiatives, their interrelationships, and their linkages to federal programs.

A few words of caution are in order at the outset. First, "soil and water conservation" refers primarily to soil erosion and management of overland flow on agricultural land. This is not to minimize at all groundwater contamination, salinity problems, flood control, urban land disturbances, and other issues within the broader scope of soil and water conservation.

Second, there are many generalizations herein about the way soil and water conservation programs are organized and operated. In fact, there is considerable variation in these programs among states and localities. Some arrangements viewed as novel here may actually be well established in some places.

Third, following various commentators (1, 6, 8, 9, 32), the assumption here is that off-site impacts of erosion are important concerns of soil and water conservation programs. This view is not universal (15).

Finally, the intent is not to forecast future developments. Rather, the focus is to identify plausible opportunities for change in soil and water conservation programs.

A program overview[1]

Current soil and water conservation programs stem from two federal initiatives taken during the Great Depression. The Soil Conservation Service and the Conservation Operations Program were created to provide technical assistance to farmers. The Agricultural Conservation Program, administered by a forerunner of today's Agricultural Stablilization and Conservation Service, was established to help farmers pay for certain farm improvements.[2] Together, these programs channeled federal funds and jobs to rural areas desperately short of both. Because the programs were intended, in large measure, to stabilize or raise rural incomes, emphasis was placed on making the program available everywhere and getting many farmers involved.[3]

To receive federal technical subsidies, states authorized the creation of soil and water conservation districts as local counterparts to SCS offices. Conservation districts typically are organized by county. They are supposed to generate local enthusiasm for soil and water conservation and set priorities for local SCS offices. Some states also grant them taxing and land use control powers (12, 20). ASCS activities are overseen by local advisory committees that have no statutory power.

The emphasis of the conservation operations program and ACP and their relation to state and local agencies are evident in funding patterns and reports of program accomplishments. Until recently, federal expenditures for soil and water conservation greatly exceeded state and local expenditures. As a result, federal agencies have tended to lead conservation efforts and set the priorities rather than to receive direction from state and local counterparts. Federal soil and water conservation funds have been apportioned among states and counties according to farm population, acreage, erodi-

---

[1] More complete discussions of the history of soil and water conservation programs are provided by 4, 14, 21, 41.

[2] ASCS has administered most but not all federal soil and water conservation cost-sharing programs. A major exception is the Great Plains Conservation Program, for which SCS administers funds.

[3] The main organizational controversy at the inception of federal soil and water conservation programs was within the U.S. Department of Agriculture. The Cooperative Extension Service sought to administer soil and water conservation functions and fought against the formation of separate bureaus with structures parallel to its own.

ble acreage, or other criteria that emphasize rural demographics rather than soil and water conservation needs. In addition, federal conservation offices are maintained in virtually all counties of every state. Program efforts have been spread thinly and widely as a result. This funding pattern has been reinforced by a progress reporting system that stresses the number of participants, acres treated, and tons of soil saved. Only the latter indicator relates to resource degradation, but it provides no information about the costs or importance of saving those tons.

In summary, the key historical elements of soil and water conservation programs have included (1) emphasis on farm income enhancement; (2) primacy of federal programs; (3) emphasis on formula funding and subsidies; (4) state and local facilitation of federal programs, with little augmentation or redirection; and (5) voluntary participation.

The fact that soil and water conservation programs are not particularly effective in protecting soil productivity and water quality has long been recognized (14, 35, 38, 39, 41). But not until the environmental movement and legislation of the 1970s did the public become generally aware of farming's side effects. For the first time, farmers came to be widely perceived as *sources* of trouble rather than victims (1).[4] During the same period, the shortcomings of previous soil and water conservation efforts were revealed in the U.S. Department of Agriculture's first National Resources Inventory and congressionally mandated reviews of soil and water conservation programs.

More recently, in response to persistent crop surpluses and huge outlays for farm income supports, the whole fabric of social subsidies to agriculture has been severely criticized. Conservation subsidies, particularly cost-sharing, are perceived in some quarters as contributing to these problems, along with support payments, price guarantees, and loan subsidies.

Environmental concerns and declining support for agricultural subsidies have shifted the political justification for soil and water conservation from supporting rural incomes to reducing the side effects of farming. Just how

---

[4] Of course, flooding, turbidity, and reservoir siltation are not new problems. The new elements are that (1) potentially dangerous chemicals have been added to the brew; (2) most people no longer have direct connections to farms, so there is less of a sense that the population of polluters overlaps greatly with the victim population (if that were the case, internalization would be achieved in a crude sense); and (3) general affluence has brought an increased emphasis on environmental quality and integrity. Due to these factors, environmental problems due to agriculture have come to be viewed as more urgent and as matters for governmental intervention rather than problems that farmers can resolve with governmental assistance.

significant the shift is can be gauged by two provisions in the Food Security Act of 1985. The conservation reserve provision authorizes USDA to pay farmers to put land into cover crops and trees that are not harvested for 10 years (13, 26, 33). Only highly erodible land is eligible. This is quite a departure from a system that has extended conservation services for virtually all land, erodible or not. Furthermore, farmers must bid for annual payments and USDA has discretion over which bids to accept. Bidding for assistance signals a fundamental shift in the relationship of federal conservation programs to farmers. Economic criteria are being used explicitly for the first time in determining who will receive conservation assistance.

A second provision, authorizing conservation compliance, calls for farmers with highly erodible cropland to implement conservation plans in order to remain eligible for loan subsidies and commodity program benefits (2, 29). For the first time, USDA income support programs will have an explicit tie to resource protection considerations.[5]

As these new provisions indicate, soil and water conservation programs are changing. In an effort to adapt to a new mix of goals and new constituencies, standards of evaluation must change; new ways of providing services must be tested; and relations between federal, state, and local jurisdictions must be restructured. Clearly, these challenges already are leading to reorganization of soil and water conservation programs. Further changes are likely to follow.

Principles of intergovernmental relations

Governments are often assumed to have three basic economic objectives: providing public goods and resolving externalities (subsummed in an efficiency objective), achieving an equitable distribution of income, and maintaining stability and justice in the marketplace (22, 23). Attainment of these goals depends in part on the organization of responsibilities among government units.

The matter of efficiency. An institutional arrangement is efficient if it responds to individuals' preferences, minimizes externalities, takes advantage of economies of scale in producing public services, and encourages

---

[5] It can be argued that cropland set-aside requirements have served resource protection goals. However, virtually any land could be set aside; it did not have to meet any conservation criteria.

innovation.[6] The first and last characteristics are usually associated with decentralized decision-making, that is, arrangements that permit maximum latitude for private decisions and take advantage of the creative forces of competition. The second and third characteristics are typically associated with centralized decision-making that internalizes spillover costs and benefits and realizes scale economies in production.

The first two characteristics are often combined in the principle of *fiscal equivalence*. This principle holds that efficient intergovernmental relations minimize externalities of making public decisions (for example, losses to the losers of majority votes) as well as those due to costs and benefits that spread beyond decision-making boundaries. Accordingly, matters of purely local or individual interest should be left exclusively to local governments or individuals. Individual or local actions that create significant externalities, either positive or negative, should be dealt with by more inclusive decision units.

There are two ways for more inclusive jurisdictions to contend with spillovers among component units. One is to assert direct administrative control. For example, this approach is taken in federal control of interstate commerce and navigation and in some environmental pollution programs. It generally ensures that action will be taken to resolve externalities, but at a cost of imposing uniform standards on affected parties.

The second approach to coordination is to provide incentives to decentralized decision units. The incentives may be fiscal or regulatory. Fiscal incentives, in the form of taxes, subsidies, or cross-compliance, encourage jurisdictions to take actions on externalities, but final authority remains decentralized. Fiscal incentives essentially alter the cost to affected governmental units of specific types of programs. They can be distorted, for example, as state or local governments substitute federal funds for their own expenditures.[7] Guarding against distortions is a major challenge confronting the use of fiscal incentives. Regulatory incentives establish standards to which decentralized units must conform. Penalties are prescribed for nonconformance. As in the case of fiscal incentives, however, actual decisions about compliance are left to the decentralized units. State pollution control mandates usually take this form.

---

[6] Oates (*23*) presented a thorough treatment of the economic approach to intergovernmental relations.

[7] Oates (*24*) found that the overall effect of intergovernmental grants is positive; that is, general public sector spending is stimulated by such grants. However, the full effect is probably diffused across several programs, of which only certain ones are targets of the grants.

In summary, fiscal equivalence is achieved with intergovernmental arrangements that balance decision-making costs against costs of externalities that remain unresolved. Such arrangements often entail a web of administrative, fiscal, and regulatory mechanisms for coordinating a hierarchy of private, local, state, and federal jurisdictions.

Finally, on the issue of supply costs, provision of public services by a centralized or multipurpose source frequently can reduce costs due to economies of scale or scope (*30*). However, through contracts with private providers or other jurisdictions, decentralized units can take advantage of such cost savings while retaining essential autonomy (*34*).[8] The preparation of soil surveys by SCS, paid for in part by local governments, is a time-honored case in point.[9] Such arrangements are increasingly common for tax collection, environmental monitoring, energy service dispatching, waste disposal, police protection, and other governmental functions.

Redistribution of income. Income redistribution is difficult to deal with in a decentralized system; those who stand to lose can easily move outside a local jurisdiction while beneficiaries move in. Moreover, competition among communities may lead to specialization in public services and, as a result, relatively income-homogeneous communities with little scope for redistribution (*24*). States are less vulnerable to the impacts of mobility or forces of specialization, and the federal government is even less hampered. Most redistributive programs must, therefore, be centralized.

It is one thing to generalize about how jurisdictions should be aligned to achieve efficiency and equity and another thing to design programs. Intergovernmental arrangements are products of diverse historical, constitutional, and political forces as well as normative economic considerations like those noted above. Nevertheless, these economic principles are important, and they have implications for soil and water conservation programs.

Program organization and administration

Of the principles indentified above, fiscal equivalence and production economies are particularly helpful in contemplating soil and water conserva-

---

[8] Chicoine and Walzer (*7*) found that agglomeration of government functions has no clear impact on the quality and costs of public services. That is, supplying services through many small, specialized units of government does not produce outcomes appreciably different from those realized with consolidated, multifunctional government.

[9] In addition to making efficient use of SCS technical expertise, the surveys produce data that are reasonably uniform within and among states and, hence, useful for state or national resource inventories and research.

tion program renovations. Several changes would promote these characteristics in soil and water conservation programs and, consequently, warrant consideration as renovation blueprints are developed.

Fiscal equivalence. The shift in policy emphasis toward the resource degradation effects of farming and away from rural income enhancement has major implications for the organization of soil and water conservation programs. Generally, the shift means that decentralized decision-making units should play greater roles (relative to their roles in redistributive programs) because of the wide variation from place to place in soil and water conservation problems and priorities. Greater local automony and leadership are important elements of an efficiency-oriented soil and water conservation program structure. Local problems will continue to have regional and national impacts, however, so mechanisms must be found for addressing these impacts without stifling local authority. The following list (not intended to be exhaustive) suggests design elements that would foster decentralized leadership within a coordinated system of national, regional, local, and private actions:

1. Limit federal technical subsidies. The availability of free technical service from SCS has obviated the need for state, local, or private sources of these services. It has had the side effect of discouraging innovative or locally appropriate remedies.[10] On the other hand, it helps control quality. There is no reason to believe that the services are provided more efficiently by SCS than they would be by private or local government sources, and some reason to believe that current arrangements are less efficient than they should be.[11] Reducing the availability of these federal services would encourage the development of decentralized sources, particularly by private farm management firms.[12] Quality con-

---

[10] SCS maintains a technical handbook for each state and each county. The handbook specifies the management practices acceptable for particular situations. Many federal and state conservation program benefits are contingent on SCS approval of the management plan, so plans that do not conform to handbook specifications are rarely proposed or approved.

[11] The somewhat outdated General Accounting Office (*38, 39*) and USDA (*37*) reports certainly raise these suspicions. More fundamentally, current programs are not disciplined by the forces of competition and are encumbered by the perversities of other farm programs. Decentralization could enhance competitive forces and loosen the ties between soil and water conservation and other farm programs.

[12] This also implies that the services would no longer be provided without charge. Cost-sharing formulas could be adjusted to compensate landowners partly or fully for planning costs.

trol responsibilities could be assumed by conservation districts, with periodic audits by state agencies or SCS.[13]

As a practical matter, moving away from a single source of technical services may be unavoidable in the near future if more states enact erosion control programs and the conservation compliance program comes off as planned.[14] Unless Congress increases the budget for conservation planning and verification, changes the conservation compliance provision, or makes commodity and loan programs significantly less attractive, it seems unlikely that SCS will be able to handle the added workload.

2. Organize local efforts by "problemsheds." It has long been recognized that county organization of soil and water conservation programs does not align well with conservation problems that cross county lines. Now that the spillovers inherent in these problems are being accorded greater importance, it makes sense to reconsider the spatial alignments of soil and water conservation programs. Some state branches of SCS are converting to a watershed or aquifer orientation for their record keeping and planning efforts (*17*). The next step would be to reconstitute the soil and water conservation delivery system and conservation districts, both on a "problemshed" level. Nebraska, for example, has consolidated soil and water conservation responsibilities in 24 natural resource districts that conforms roughly to important hydrologic subdivisions of the state (*19*).

3. Enhance local accountability. Nonfarm groups have affirmative interests in redressing external impacts of farming, such as water pollution and reduction of wildlife habitat. Because nonfarm groups bear a large share of the costs of solving soil and water conservation problems, fiscal equivalence clearly calls for them to be involved in program decision-making. Moreover, unless nonfarm constituencies can be engaged constructively, farmers stand to lose valuable help in protecting their land and water resources.

Several organizational forms can foster that engagement. One is selection of conservation district members in general elections. This can make

[13] Breimeyer (*6*) has suggested that quality control and enforcement roles, much like the roles of commodity and food inspection programs, may become the core of federal soil and water conservation programs in the future.

[14] Illinois, Iowa, Ohio, and South Dakota have erosion control laws for farmland. Many states require erosion to be controlled at construction sites. In most cases, conservation districts and SCS play important roles in approving erosion control plans. Conservation compliance requires that by 1990 applicants for farm program assistance must have SCS-approved conservation plans for their "highly erodible land" in order to qualify. By the mid-1990s, only farmers who have fully implemented their conservation plans will qualify for federal farm programs.

soil and water conservation programs more visible to the nonfarm electorate. Nonfarm involvement could be ensured by designating seats on conservation district boards for population centers within a district's jurisdiction.

4. Augment local powers. The shift from public assistance toward public health and welfare purposes suggests the need for additional policy tools. Regulation, eminent domain, and tax collection powers all have roles to play. Where landowners cannot be persuaded to reduce serious sediment losses, for example, conservation districts may need access to regulatory or eminent domain powers. Moreover, if conservation districts are to assume leadership responsibilities, they need taxing powers to provide an independent fiscal base. Some states accord such powers to conservation districts, although they are rarely used. Other states limit district powers or impose stiff local referendum requirements. Such constraints impede the development of forceful local soil and water conservation programs.

5. Replace formula funding with grant support. Solving resource degradation problems is a dynamic process. It requires the ability to direct resources to the most pressing problems and move resources as priorities change, old problems are solved, and new problems emerge.[15] Formula funding greatly reduces the flexibility to move resources. Grant funding is much more flexible. In addition, by requiring matching contributions, grants can be used to encourage local leadership of and resource commitments to soil and water conservation programs. For many reasons, therefore, increased emphasis on grant funding of soil and water conservation is warranted.

This has already been recognized: USDA aims to target 25 percent of its soil and water conservation expenditures, largely through matching and block grant programs (*3*); and several states employ grant programs in allocating soil and water conservation program and cost-sharing funds. For example, 50 percent of Illinois' outlays are made in this way (*16*). Further movement in this direction at both the federal and state levels may be needed.[16]

---

[15] Focusing resources on the most pressing problems is the gist of targeting, a concept only recently discovered in connection with conservation programs and now a major force in them (*25, 27, 28, 31, 35, 36*).

[16] Nominal state and local contributions to soil and water conservation programs increased about 60 percent between 1975 and 1985, according to Eugene Lamb with the National Association of Conservation Districts, versus an increase of about 40 percent in federal contributions (*40*). According to the president's 1986 budget, federal soil and water conservation outlays are scheduled to decline in coming years. Whether those projections come true or not, the trend is clearly toward an increasing state and local share of soil and water conservation expenditures. Thus, in years ahead, state adoption of the matching grant approach may be especially consequential.

6. Apportion costs in line with benefits. A corollary to fiscal equivalence is that those who reap benefits from public services should pay a proportionate share of the costs. Matching grants are one way to ensure that local or state governments are bearing part of the burden for soil and water conservation, from which they will gain through better water quality, more efficient farms, and so forth. However, strict matching formulae artificially limit the incidence of costs, while the distribution of benefits varies widely from project to project. A more efficient system would allow applicants to make cost-share rate proposals as part of their bids for grants. Among two local projects offering comparable benefits, for example, a state or federal agency could select the one for which local sources are willing to bear more of the costs. This is already possible in most federal and state grant programs, but minimum cost-share levels are usually specified and applicants typically propose the minimum.

Two ambitious approaches to cost allocation have already been tried and deserve further consideration. One is bidding, as with the CRP. Competitive bidding should lead applicants to reveal the lowest payments for which they will participate. This approach requires that the projects be divisible into groups, within which the nonlocal benefits are relatively homogeneous. It also requires that each group has enough bids to be competitive.[17] These requirements suggest that bidding is not applicable for all soil and water conservation programs and may be more suitable at the state and federal levels than for local jurisdictions.

The second approach is variable cost-sharing, such as ASCS has tried on an experimental basis (*27*). Higher cost-share rates were offered for practices that accomplished large reductions in soil erosion or protected "critical" land. These criteria are crude indicators of off-site benefits at best, and they indicate nothing about benefits on-site, for which landowners might be expected to pay. Better variable cost-share criteria would introduce economic considerations. If bidding cannot be used to elicit basic economic information, then simulation models might provide generic information

---

[17] It is possible to link decision levels through a bid system by allowing each level (below the grant agency) to specify its willingness to contribute. Using the conservation reserve for illustration, a landowner might bid $60 per acre, and it might be worth $10 per acre to the conservation district and $5 to the state to have that land enrolled. These contributions could be rolled into the farmer's bid, producing a net bid of $45/acre. That bid would be more competitive in the federal program. Such a system would permit local and state government participation in what is essentially a federally administered farmer bid program. Evidence that such participation may be attractive is present in Illinois, where several private lake associations and at least one municipal water utility are supplementing federal and state cost-sharing for sediment reduction measures on farms (*10*).

on which to base cost-share rates for particular practices (*4, 11, 18*).

A third, untried opportunity for apportioning costs involves funding cost-sharing out of water use fees (or charges on pollution). Surcharges might be added to boating, fishing, and waterfowl hunting licenses; hunting ammunition; water bills; tillage equipment prices; and so forth to finance the public share of measures to reduce off-site impacts of farming. It is inappropriate to base public contributions on these sources alone because they do not cover the full range of benefits or beneficiaries. But they do provide a way to have some important classes of beneficiaries pay a larger share of the costs.

7. Develop regional program infrastructure. Any decentralized organization of soil and water conservation programs, by county or problemshed, will still exhibit spillovers. This means states and the federal government inevitably will need to address problems that cross jurisdictions. States have sufficient powers to contend with transboundary problems within their borders. The federal government is far less able to contend with interstate problems. Yet, challenges similar to those presently being addressed in the Chesapeake Bay region must be faced in many areas around the country (e.g., the Columbia, Mississippi, Missouri, and Tennessee River Basins). Thus, it will be important to develop infrastructure for addressing regional problems, and the federal government must provide the leadership.[18]

Efficient production. The second set of changes aims to consolidate and economize on the production of soil and water conservation services. Currently, those services are delivered through four overlapping systems: SCS, ASCS, conservation districts, and the Cooperative Extension Service. There are undoubtedly opportunities to simplify and consolidate. Following are two possibilities:

8. Consolidate local services in conservation districts and private sources. As local planning and management capabilities are enhanced, conservation districts and private farm managers will become capable of providing many services traditionally supplied by SCS and Cooperative Extension agents. In addition to technical advice and plannings, districts could be contracted to handle local arrangements for other federal programs.[19] These

---

[18] Since the decline of the regional river basin initiatives of the 1960s, federal powers over environmental protection have been strengthened considerably. These powers may provide the basis for regional infrastructures to deal with soil and water conservation problems.

[19] To encourage private sources of technical and planning services, charges would need to be made for conservation district services.

changes would allow significant reductions in the SCS and ASCS delivery systems. They also imply changes in the relationships between Cooperative Extension and conservation districts at the state level.

9. *Consolidate basic information collection and research at the federal level.* Data on the conditions of soil and water resources and fundamental knowledge about resource management, hydrology, and soil science are needed for a variety of soil and water conservation purposes. With regard to the data, it is important that they be collected in uniform ways and remain accessible. For these reasons, centralization makes sense. Current arrangements, in which local or state jurisdictions share the costs of soil surveys, need not be changed appreciably. Concerning research, SCS, the Agricultural Research Service, and the experiment station system (Cooperative States Research Service) all are involved. Redundancies and administrative costs could probably be reduced without appreciably affecting research innovation. But clearly, federal leadership must be maintained because subfederal jurisdictions are less likely to support basic research.[20]

The search for efficiency

A search for greater efficiency seems to characterize the policy environment for soil and water conservation programs. This has important implications for soil and water conservation program organization. It suggests, among other things, the need to strengthen private and local roles in program implementation, curb redundancies in the delivery system, and develop new and innovative ways of sharing program costs.

The measures outlined above should be viewed as opportunities, not as forecasts of things to come. No effort has been made to assess their political potential. Undoubtedly, many would not appeal to significant interest groups. Perhaps more important is to recognize that the suggestions collectively anticipate fundamental changes in the roles conservation agencies play and, hence, in their interrelationships. Such changes would require legislative action, starting with Congress. As evident from the CRP and conservation compliance provisions in the 1985 farm bill, fundamental changes in farm programs are possible in the current policy environment. The time is right to consider opportunities and ideas for shaping future conservation programs.

---

[20] This is not to disregard the importance of state contributions to experiment stations, which provide a valuable, decentralized link in the current research enterprise.

REFERENCES

1. Batie, Sandra A. 1985. *Environmental limits: The new constraints.* Issues in Science and Technology (Fall): 134-143.
2. Benbrook, Charles E. 1980. *Integrating soil conservation and commodity programs: A policy proposal.* Journal of Soil and Water Conservation 34(4): 160-167.
3. Block, John R. 1982. *Remarks.* In Proceedings, 36th Annual Convention. National Association of Conservation Districts, Washington, D.C.
4. Braden, John B., Gary V. Johnson, and Diane G. Martin. 1985. *Efficient control of agricultural sediment deposition in water courses.* In Theodore M. Shad [editor] *Options for Reaching Water Quality Goals.* American Water Resources Association, Bethesda, Maryland. pp. 69-76.
5. Braden, John B., and Donald L. Uchtmann. 1982-1983. *Soil conservation amidst faltering environmental commitments and the "New Federalism."* Boston College Environmental Affairs Law Review 10(3): 639-696.
6. Breimeyer, Harold F. 1985. *Soil conservation institutions of the future.* Journal of Soil and Water Conservation 40(1): 182.
7. Chicoine, David L., and Norman Walzer. 1985. *Government structure and local public finance.* Oelgeschlager, Gunn, and Hain, Inc., Boston, Massachusetts.
8. Clark, Edwin H., II, Jennifer A. Haverkamp, and William Chapman. 1985. *Eroding soils: The off-farm impacts.* Conservation Foundation, Washington, D.C.
9. Crosson, Pierre. 1984. *New Perspectives on soil conservation policy.* Journal of Soil and Water Conservation 39(4): 222-225.
10. Daily, David. 1986. *Erosion control plan for the Dunlap Lake drainage basin: Supplement.* Madison County Soil and Water Conservation District, Edwardsville, Illinois.
11. Eleveld, Bartlelt, Gary V. Johnson, and Robert Dumsday. 1983. *SOILEC: Simulating the economics of soil conservation.* Journal of Soil and Water Conservation 38(5): 387-389.
12. Garner, Mary M. 1977. *Regulatory programs for nonpoint pollution control: The role of conservation districts.* Journal of Soil and Water Conservation 32(4): 199-204.
13. Heimlich, Ralph E. 1986. *Reducing erosion and agricultural capacity: Our cropland base and the conservation reserve.* Economic Research Service, U.S. Department of Agriculture, Washington, D.C.
14. Held, R.B., and Marion Clawson. 1965. *Soil conservation in perspective.* The John Hopkins University Press, Baltimore, Maryland.
15. Howe, Richard S. 1985. *The politics of nonpoint pollution control: A local perspective.* Journal of Soil and Water Conservation 40(1): 107.
16. Illinois Department of Agriculture. 1985. *T by 2000.* Springfield, Illinois.
17. Illinois Department of Agriculture, Division of Natural Resources. 1986. *1986 annual progress report.* Springfield, Illinois.
18. Knisel, W.G., editor. 1980. *CREAMS: A field scale model for chemicals, runoff, and erosion from agricultural management systems.* Conservation Research Report No. 20. U.S. Department of Agriculture, Washington, D.C.
19. Marlette, R.. and C.L. Williams. 1979. *Nebraska multi-purpose resources districts.* In *Legal, Institutional, and Social Aspects of Irrigation and Drainage and Water Resources Planning and Management.* American Society of Civil Engineers, New York, New York. pp. 266-81.
20. Massey, Dean T. 1983-1984. *Land use regulatory power of conservation districts in the midwestern states for controlling nonpoint source pollution.* Drake Law Review 33: 35-111.

21. Morgan, R. 1965. *Governing soil conservation*. The John Hopkins University Press, Baltimore, Maryland.

22. Musgrave, Richard. 1959. *The theory of public finance*. McGraw-Hill Book, New York, New York.

23. Oates, Wallace E. 1972. *Fiscal federalism*. Harcourt Brace Jovanovich, New York, New York.

24. Oates, Wallace E. 1985. *Searching for leviathan: An empirical study*. American Economic Review 75(4): 748-757.

25. Ogg, Clayton W., James D. Johnson, and Kenneth C. Clayton. 1982. *A policy option for targeting soil conservation expenditures*. Journal of Soil and Water Conservation 37(2): 68-72.

26. Ogg, Clayton W., Shwu-Eng Webb, and Wen-Yuan Huang. 1984. *Cropland acreage reduction alternatives: An economic analysis of soil conservation reserve and competitive bids*. Journal of Soil and Water Conservation 39(6): 379-383.

27. Park, William M., and David G. Sawyer. 1985. *Targeting soil erosion control efforts in a critical watershed*. Staff Report No. AGES850801. Economic Research Service, U.S. Department of Agriculture, Washington, D.C.

28. Raitt, Daryll D. 1986. *Economic impact of the conservation targeting program: Daviess and Harrison Counties, Missouri*. Staff Report No. AGES850903. Economic Research Service, U.S. Department of Agriculture, Washington, D.C.

29. Reichelderfer, Katherine H. 1985. *Do USDA farm program participants contribute to soil erosion?* Agricultural Economics Report No. 532. Economic Research Service, U.S. Department of Agriculture, Washington, D.C.

30. Rothenberg, Jerome. 1970. *Local decentralization and the theory of optimal government*. In Julius Margolis [editor] *The Analysis of Public Output*. National Bureau of Economic Research, New York, New York. pp. 31-64.

31. Runge, C. F., W.E. Larson, and G. Roloff. 1986. *Using productivity measures to target conservation programs: A comparative anaylsis*. Journal of Soil and Water Conservation 41(1): 45-49.

32. Swanson, Earl R. 1979. *Economic evaluation of soil erosion: Productivity losses and off-site damages*. Staff Paper No. 79-E-77. Department of Agricultural Economics, University of Illinois, Urbana.

33. Taff, Steve, and C. Ford Runge. 1986. *Supply control, conservation and budget restraint: Conflicting instruments in the 1985 farm bill*. Staff Paper No. P86-33. Department of Agricultural and Applied Economics, University of Minnesota, St. Paul.

34. Tullock, Gordon. 1969. *Federalism: Problems of scale*. Public Choice 6(Spring): 19-29.

35. U.S. Department of Agriculture. 1982. *A national program for soil and water conservation*. Washington, D.C.

36. U.S. Department of Agriculture. 1986. *An economic analysis of USDA erosion control programs: A new perspective*. Agricultural Economic Report No. 560. Washington, D.C.

37. U.S. Department of Agriculture, Agricultural Stabilization and Conservation Service. 1980. *National summary evaluation of the Agricultural Conservation Program, phase I*. Washington, D.C.

38. U.S. General Accounting Office. 1977. *To protect tomorrow's food supply, soil conservation needs priority attention*. CED 77-30. Washington, D.C.

39. U.S. General Accounting Office. 1983. *Agricultural's soil conservation programs miss full potential in the fight against soil erosion*. GAO/RCED-84-48. Washington, D.C.

40. U.S. Office of Management and Budget. Annual. *Budget of the U.S. Government.* U.S. Government Printing Office. Washington, D.C.
41. Williams, Craig L. 1979. *Soil conservation and water pollution control: The muddy record of the United States Department of Agriculture.* Boston College Environmental Affairs Law Review 7(3): 365-421.

Index

equation for (WEQ), 19, 34
in Great Plains, 16
landscape factors, 20
Wisconsin, 142
conservation districts abolished, 140
CRP participation, 148
Farmland Preservation Program, 144
program redirection in, 145
research council, 147
soil conservation organization, 141
Soil Erosion Control Program, 142
zoning program, 139